COPING WITH STRESS
AND
BUILDING LEADERSHIP

Copyright © 2011 Melvin Mahone

All rights reserved. Printed in the U.S.A.

No part of this publication may be reproduced or transmitted in any form or by any means, electronic or mechanical, including photocopy, recording or any information storage and retrieval system now known or to be invented, without permission in writing from the publisher, except by a reviewer who wishes to quote brief passages in connection with a review written for inclusion in a magazine, newspaper or broadcast.

Published in the United States by
Beckham Publications Group, Inc.
P.O. Box 4066, Silver Spring, MD 20914

ISBN: 978-0-9848243-2-8

COPING WITH STRESS AND BUILDING LEADERSHIP

ONE MAN'S JOURNEY

Melvin Mahone, PhD

PUBLICATIONS GROUP, INC.
Silver Spring

Contents

Acknowledgments 7

Introduction 9

Chapter 1: The Mahone Family and the Early Years that Shaped My Adulthood. 11

Chapter 2: Stress in the Workplace 31

Chapter 3: Leadership in the Workplace 49

Chapter 4: Success Through Positive Thinking 98

Chapter 5: Motivation and Get Motivated 122

Chapter 6: Inspiration About Life. 130

Chapter 7: Being a Bureaucrat and in Government Employment 150

Chapter 8: Final Observations. 170

Epilogue. 179

Notes 189

Bibliography. 191

Acknowledgments

This book is dedicated to the thousands of personnel in law enforcement all over the world. It is dedicated to the politicians I pray for everyday of the week that they will not do to another private citizen who was concerned about the well-being of the community by volunteering for both parties the way that they did me. They made me homeless three times. I volunteered with the Republicans and the Democrats. I am proud to be a Centrist.

Furthermore, I would like to dedicate this book to my mother, Mrs. Betty Mahone Dermer, Ms. Betty Mahone Curtis, and the rest of my family who helped me find myself and overcome a stress-related condition so I could become a productive citizen once again. And thanks to all the people reflected in these pages that I leaned on and have been inspired by. From them, I gained the strength and fortitude to lead.

Introduction

What do you say about a person who has wanted to become a law enforcement bureaucrat since his childhood, but as he grew older could not pursue his goal because of a post-traumatic stress condition? This is my predicament. And it began when I was a marine stationed in Vietnam. My condition became more intense later. I left the US Marine Corp and became a police officer, customs aide, and correctional treatment specialist. Then I earned a Ph.D. degree while working long hours to support my family. I had endured various levels of stress in those law enforcement positions before finally leaving the federal prison system in 1980.

Since I have both practical experience and teaching experience in law enforcement and have served in the military, I have a vested interest in the law enforcement community. Post-traumatic stress disorder and depression are common afflictions with law enforcement personnel. Therefore I want to tell my story to the thousands of law enforcement personnel who may also suffer from this crippling condition that affects millions on a regular basis.

I began my employment with the federal government with the US Protective Service as a United States Federal Special Police in 1971. I worked many hours attending . I continued to go to school on a full-time basis when I transferred to the United States Customs Service from 1972 until 1977. I worked an average of 12 to 13 hours a day with the Customs Service while attending college. In 1978, I transferred to the

United States Department of Justice in Milan, Michigan, as a correctional officer. I stayed there for a year. By this time, I had earned a master's degree. I was promoted to correctional treatment specialist since transferring to the Metropolitan Correctional Center Chicago in 1979. Here, I continued to work long hours.

In September 1980, I was forced to resign from the MCC Chicago, because I was burned out. I suffered from depression. I suffered from paranoia. I suffered from PTSD. At the time, psychiatrists and psychologists said that I could never work again. MCC Chicago offered me disability but I did not accept the benefits. I was in denial. I was lost in the wilderness. I did not have anyone to think for me. During that time, I was so numbed that I did not have any feelings at all—forget love or affection. I had an increased form of an exaggerated startled response called hypervigilantism, and a sleeping disorder. I found out very quickly that reactions to stress vary among individuals because perceptions of situations are subjective.

I was homeless intermittently from 1987 until 1994. I lived on and off with relatives and in homeless shelters until my mental condition was stabilized in 1997 and again in 2000. The Veterans Administration medications improved my mental picture and condition. There is nothing like having an eye-opening experience to share with others so they might not have to suffer or go through what you went through. I promised myself that if I ever got on my feet, I was going to help every law enforcement officer that I could. And I have. Over the years, I have shared with the CIA, the FBI, and various players in the law enforcement field about stress and how it leads to mental illnesses. God Bless America!

Chapter

1

The Mahone Family and the Early Years that Shaped My Adulthood

On October 7, 1951, I was born to Mr. and Mrs. Elbert Mahone Sr., in Chicago, Illinois. In 1954, we moved from public housing on the West Side of Chicago to 1537 South Hamlin Ave. I was the sixth of 10 children in my family. My mother had a sixth grade education, and my father had a second grade education. My mother was a beautician and had her own business. My father worked as a steel cutter on Chicago's South Side of Chicago.

As I look back at my childhood, it was a happy one. I was bullied all the time in school because I was skinny and underweight. I got good grades up until the time that I left high school in 1968. The roughness of the gangs became too much so I left school.

My father, Elbert Mahone Sr., was born to Alec and Ada Mahone on September 25, 1914, in Columbus, Georgia. My father was strict and had a nervous condition that precluded him from driving and holding down employment that was stressful. He worked at Siegel Steel Company for 20 years.

My father was also a minister and he named his church The Straight Gate Spiritual Church. The church was located in our basement and our family went to church two times a week; we attended church religiously on Sundays.

My father was a disciplinarian, and he would use a switch and hit all 10 of us children, usually with our clothes off. Sometimes, our skin would bruise. He was a brutal man; he would read the Bible and recite scripture while he was beating us with an ironing cord. My mother tried to intercede on numerous occasions, but to no avail she could not stop the extreme cruelty done by my father to his children.

My father was not only cruel to his children, but he was also cruel to my mother. He hit her on numerous occasions; on one occasion, he hit her with a frying (skillet) pan, causing her eyes to swell and her face to turn red and blue colors.

Mainly though, my father was a good provider, working hard and supporting his family. He was morally a good man, but he had violent ways. My father was a good leader because he taught positive values to his children by being employed, being honest, religious, and by being firm but fair Eventually, my mother lost her feelings for him because of his cruelty both to his children and to her. My mother told us on numerous occasions to not treat our wives the way that our father treated her.

My mother, Betty, was born to Robert and Eva Hanks in Starkville, Mississippi, on February 3, 1920. She grew up in Starkville and also in Centralia, Illinois. I have a good mother who has good and decent ways about her. She has always been there when I needed her. If I need a loan, she is there. If I need money for gas, she is there. She is always there to give me intelligent advice and she has an excellent memory. My mother constantly wears a smile on her face and has never been cruel to me knowingly.

There difference between my mother and my father is like the difference between night and day. Even though my father was a good provider, my mother was a better provider than my father. I will never forget how on Easter Sundays each and every year, my mother would always buy name brands and brand-new clothes from a quality clothing store. My father would buy clothes and shoes from a secondhand garage sale. He would always be looking for a better deal in Mr. Davis's garage. My mother and he would argue about these clothing purchases every holiday.

At Christmas, we all had a good holiday. I always knew that I would have several gifts beneath the tree in our living room; gifts that my mother's money bought, not my father's. He was cheap. He never, ever—to the best of my recollection—gave me any money out of his pocket to spend on myself. He would always make an excuse not to give me any money. He would say, "You have food in the refrigerator at home, you don't need any money." My mother understood us when we wanted a treat such as Sir Chicken, who specialized in chicken wings, so she would give each child $5.00 spending money.

My mother earned more money than my father. My mother, in the 1950s until the 1980s, made $50,000.00 annually since she ran her own beauty shop. My father only made $10,000.00 a year during those years, which left my mother saddled with paying most of the bills. Even though we had our own two-flat building, we never were out of doors or out of food. I can always remember on Mondays, my mother would prepare a big dinner for the entire family because that was her day off work.

My mother was, and still is, the backbone of the family. She was a leader, the breadwinner; she was a disciplinarian as well, but she was never was brutal like my father. She would calmly talk to you about what you had done wrong instead of giving you a beating. My mother, to this day, still talks about how abusive my father was to her and to his children. She has said on more than one occasion, "We all could have been hurt or killed, as a result of his violent temper." I love my mother. She holds a special place in my heart. She is 91-years-old now, and on many occasions she has said she wants to live to be one hundred. I am a positive thinker, and

I believe that she will live far beyond 100-years-old. She is in good shape and looks like she is 60 years of age. The first child born within wedlock to Elbert Sr. and Betty Mahone was Elbert Mahone Jr. My brother was born on January 18,1939. Junior, as we called him, was young and ruthless. He didn't care about anybody. He always wanted something for nothing and could never hold down a job for any length of time. After he married, he was a wife beater. He was verbally abusive to my mother; and for a time, he was like that toward my father, until he realized that he needed him to take away my mother and father's home from them. To this day, my sister-in-law has a house that she did not pay for at all. My brother was a user and would always say, "You are a fool for working, I'm never going to work." When he was in his early twenties, my father made him pay rent while he lived at our abode on the West Side of Chicago and provide a living for his children.

My father and Junior got into many arguments about his not working, so eventually Junior took found work driving cabs. He gambled and was not doing much of anything with his life. He and his wife had several children while he lived with my family on the first floor of our house. My brothers and I had to sleep in the kitchen on a rollaway bed to accommodate him and his family. He was less than a man.

Prior to the death of his son, Elbert made amends with his son about employment, and other problems that they argued about in the pass. Elbert Jr. preceded Elbert Sr. in death by suffering a massive heart attack. He was only 56 years old. My mother always said that he died young because he disrespected his mother and took her house away from her. However, that was not the only reason he died young. He swindled money from senior citizens in the various churches that he attended. He would lie about my mother. He would do anything to make it look that he was right and everyone else was wrong.

Junior didn't work, so he never accumulated any social security. He never was a positive role model for anyone, and he used to say to me mockingly because I was always in school "You are going to be a Ph.D. and M.D." Well, one thing did happen for certain, I earned my Ph.D.; I received my degree in criminal justice and corrections. I might not have property or have accumulated monetary wealth, but I earned everything that I have and I earned it honestly.

The next sibling was James Mahone. He was the second child, born on January 19, 1941. James was a good man; he was a veteran from the United States Marine Corps. Due to various disciplinarian infractions, however, he received a less-than-honorable discharge from the Marine Corps.

Betty Mahone, born on August 29, 1942, was the third child born to the Mahone union. Betty is a kind, sweet, likeable sister. If ever you needed help with anything, she was always there to help you. She was a good parent to her children and was a good wife to her husband, although as of this writing they are in the process of getting a divorce after four decades of marriage. That is really sad since Betty really wanted her marriage to work. Her husband, it was later found out, had other children by another woman while he was still married to my sister. Betty never went outside of her marriage or cheat on her spouse. She truly believed in her marriage vows, and she tried so hard to make her marriage work no matter what. However, the marriage just was not meant to be for her.

Betty helped me immensely when I was sick due to stress. Even though I still have a post-traumatic stress and depression condition, she took the time to inform me of the symptoms and what to expect from the illness. She told me on numerous occasions that I would be chemically unbalanced and that someone would have to think for me intermittently during my lifetime. She told me that I would have to be on a special diet. She told me that not only would I have to be only a special diet, I would have to exercise. I could not drink alcohol or caffeine.

Everything that my sister told me was true. You see, I didn't say this earlier, Betty spent almost three-fourths of her life in college studying to be a nurse. She is a psychological nurse, a registered nurse, and a former administrator in human services. She holds numerous degrees and has worked hard for things she has attained. It is a shame that she had to marry someone that I believe did not appreciate her the way that a husband should after all of those years.

I stayed with my sister Betty on numerous occasions while I was recuperating from PTSD. Recently, she had brain surgery. She is almost 70 and looks 35 years younger. She is still attractive, vibrant, and appreciates and desires the finer things in life: music, food, and cultural well-being.

Delores, the fourth child, born on December 13, 1943, was a gentle giant. At times, she could be mean-spirited, but she did not mean any harm. I always played around with her as a child and would eat her food up when she would send me to a restaurant for her. Whatever the restaurant was at the time, it didn't make any difference to me. I would eat and share her food without her permission.

When we were young, I vividly remembered her hitting me with a shoe when she got mad or when I would not obey her for doing household tasks. On Saturdays, the day that everyone performed chores around our house, my father would tell Delores what needed to be done and she would delegate the tasks to the other siblings. If the tasks were not done to specification, she would throw a shoe at you. She would even take the shoe and hit you with it until you complied with her demands of scrubbing the floor correctly or doing some other household chore. That's why I call her the gentle giant. She only hit you when she felt she had to.

I also remember my sister Delores as being sickly most of her life. She had high blood pressure and could not eat pork or consume various foods that would make her e sick with different ailments. When she was an adult, I remember her getting married. The marriage didn't last longer than a week. The man she married was evil-spirited and mean, and that's why I knew that the marriage would not last. You see, my sister would have her mean-spirited days, as well. When my father was asked to come and get his daughter from a man as evil as her husband, he went with all deliberate spirit. My father loved his children in his own special way.

Delores had a son; he was above average and highly intelligent. He never cursed. He was respectable. He always obeyed his mother. Whenever asked to go on errands, he would go without fail. I called him "Mr. Glenn," as he was a man before it he had time to become grown. He took care of his mother because he never knew what it was like to have a father around the house. He moved with her to Oakland, California, where he excelled in school. He then moved with his mother to Atlanta, Georgia, and easily assimilated with the other children at his new school and in his new neighborhood.

My sister did a great job raising her son, even without the luxury of a "man" around the house. She has never asked anybody for a dime and has carried her own load. She was always employed to the best of my recollection. Delores now resides in Georgia and has accomplished a lot since being down South. She is a writer, a publisher, and a grandmother of two. She also took care of my father when he was down and out. He needed her in his weaning years before his death. He requested to be cremated and Delores obeyed his wishes. I love my sister and wish her the best in whatever she chooses to do in the very near future with her writing or publishing.

The next child born to my parents was Michael Mahone born on October 11, 1948. Michael was always giving and kindhearted. He taught me how to play sports, and I credit him as the reason I enlisted in the US Marine Corps. I wanted to follow a family tradition and also escape the local gangs that taunted me in high school. Michael was my rifle instructor in the Marine Corps. I have always respected him because he has always been someone whom I looked up to. Both of us worked in law enforcement because of our military experience. And we were close in that Michael was the fifth child born in our family and I was their sixth child.

Nadine Mahone was the seventh sibling; she was born on April 6, 1955. Nadine was nice and easygoing, clean and wholesome. She was an obedient child and never caused my parents any trouble. My mother never had to tell Nadine what to do more than once. On Saturdays, she would do her assigned cleaning task with ease. She went to school on time and came straight back home; she received good grades in school as well. At school, she was never bullied, neither did bully or fight anyone. She attended our father's church and appreciated his guidance.

She attended the Boys & Girls Clubs across the street on Hamlin and 15th. My mother and father were always proud of my sister Nadine because of the way she carried herself in public and at school.

When my sister Nadine was of age to have a boyfriend, she respected my mother and father and would never stay out late. She would always follow the rules and regulations that my parents laid down for all of the girls in the house that were dating boys.

If there were any questions or concerns regarding how to behave, Nadine went directly to our parents for guidance. When Nadine became of age to take a husband, she married Eugene Harding, who was the hardest-working man I have ever known. He was faithful, understanding, and a good role model for their three daughters.

Nadine never had to work while she was married to Eugene. She always had his dinner prepared when he came home from work. And Eugene would paint and spruce up the house when needed. He was also clean and wholesome, and he set a good example for others to follow, especially for his girls when it was time for them to marry.

Everyone was shocked, however, when Nadine's marriage failed. No one wanted to see her and Eugene get divorced, after 23 years of marriage. The pain was so much for Nadine that she never married again. Now she has to be a surrogate father to her grandchildren, and she has to work for a living since she no longer has a husband who will care for her.

Gregory was my parent's eighth child. Born on May 29, 1956, Gregory was a quiet, obedient, and intelligent boy. He was bullied sometimes in school, but he never bullied anyone. Gregory was always inquisitive as a child and would ask questions about the weirdest things. He would paint our bedroom odd colors, but for the most part he kept to himself most of his childhood. Gregory never had a desire to join the Boys & Girls Clubs. My brother never had any girlfriends nor did he have many boys that he went out with socially.

Gregory was an above-average youngster throughout school, from kindergarten through high school. He would not settle for less than an above average grade. When he became a teenager and was matriculating through high school, he was the victim of educational racism at a predominately white school. My mother had to transfer him to a more integrated high school in downtown Chicago. Jones Commercial High School was equipped with all of the latest computers and business equipment. It was there that my brother was inspired to become an entrepreneur. When he got older, he started his own business. Gregory was highly motivated, and I believe his motivation was also a result of the strict and conservative upbringing that pushed him to succeed.

Gregory was also a religious person; he became a Jehovah's Witness. When he decided to get married, he married a Jehovah's Witness and they have three daughters. His wife, Deborah, is one of sweetest people on Earth and there is always joyfulness in their household.

The average person, including myself, does not know much about or is in touch with the Jehovah's Witness faith. What is so shocking to me is the way Jehovah's Witnesses take so much mental abuse from the public when they go out to spread their ministry within communities. People would slam doors in their faces. People would spit on them, curse them, and call them names all because of their own ignorance of the Jehovah's Witness faith. There is only one God. And we should all be respectful of how someone else practices their religion and how they worship their God.

On September 14, 1955, Patricia became the ninth child to join the Mahone family. Patricia was a sight to see. She was very attractive with light complexion and long hair. She was also accident prone. At an early age, she fell from the front porch and fractured her skull; as a youngster, she received third-degree grease burns from a skillet. I felt sorry for my sister. She had so much bad luck, however, God has been with her to get her through all the trials and tribulations that she went through as she was growing up.

Patricia was also a quiet and obedient child who didn't cause my parents any problems. She didn't get any "switchings" from my father or mother. She received high marks in school and went on to college. With her current husband, Bernard Kato, she formed PBK Secretarial Limited, and their business was a smashing success. She is currently a manager in the entertainment business (Blockbuster) and the loves it. She and her husband have three children.

For Patricia, it was love at first sight with Bernie. She loved to roller skate and they met more than 40 years ago at Albany Skating Rink on the West Side of Chicago. Pat and Bernie would skate at matinees and they would go to the midnight ramble; they would also go to movies together. They grew on one another, and she met Bernie's entire family as I did during this time. I was glad that Pat and Bernie married; it agrees with them both.

Their daughter, Tiffany, is in college to become a physical trainer. Their son Patrick is in college studying to enter the personal medical field. They are both intelligent children. Lenard is living with his wife in Indianapolis and they have a beautiful son. He is involved with trucks and car repair. And they have a new dog, a German shepherd that is a sight to see for anyone's eyes. Lenard's wife is a homemaker and they plan on relocating, however, they have not decided where. They were considering Seattle, Washington.

All and all, my sister Patricia is blessed and has been through much in life. She's battled cancer and beat it; she is now living life to the fullest and I wish her and her entire family the best of luck for their future endeavors.

My sister Carolyn was the tenth and final child born into the Mahone family. Her birthdate is November 20, 1960. Being the youngest, she could've been labeled as a spoiled brat because all of her siblings spoiled her. During her childhood years, Carolyn was raised by all of us. I would take her for walks and for swing rides in the park. She posed no problems for my father or mother and the rod was spared because she was the youngest child. Carolyn was fragile and got her way more than any of us. She would always get the benefit of the doubt when there was any problem with her behavior.

Carolyn was not a disciplinary problem and always received good grades in school. All of her schoolteachers, from kindergarten to the 12th grade, got along well with her. She, on the other hand, would come home boasting about how she got over on various teachers throughout the course of her day. My mother always dressed up Carolyn. She would not get secondhand clothes from garage sales like the rest of her sisters and brothers. She would get new clothes from name-brand stores. Carolyn would even get extra allowance.

I can vividly recall my father posting a picture Carolyn painted on the basement wall for all of us to see, proud that his youngest child was doing so well in school compared to the other children. I spent quality time with my beloved sister Carolyn, but she got away with highway robbery.

Carolyn is highly intelligent and received her license to be a nurse by taking and passing the test on her first try. She is now married with an older husband who is diligent and hard working, and he is spoiling her as we did. Carolyn is a certified mortician and a nurse; her husband, Russell, is retired. He is putting their only child, Elizabeth, through college. I am so proud of both of them. She has overcome many adversities most of her adult life. She had a battle with cancer and beat it. She has battled with alcoholism and beat it. When she had a miscarriage and her baby girl was a stillbirth, Carolyn was deeply depressed for years. However, she overcame that as well.

Carolyn has found God as her savior, and since she has put God in her life she has found the extra strength needed to overcome any personal, medical, and emotional problems. God bless my sister. She has a lot of the qualities that I have.

My Children

The first child born to Grace Maxwell was Richard Maxwell. He is my birth son. Richard has been a mother's boy all of his life. He would lock himself in the basement and watch cartoons. That has been the story of his life. If I ever tried to give structure to Richard, his mother, my ex-wife, Grace, would interfere and stop me. I was strict with Richard because I wanted him to be a disciplined man. His mother, on the other hand, did not see things the same way that I did. I never abused Richard. I would give him essential chores like making up his bed and taking out the garbage. I would tell him to sweep the kitchen floor, and I'd have him mop the floors all over the house. I would give him task to perform that I believed would make him some responsibility. Despite that, his mother intervened. It was very frustrating. Well, as time progressed, Richard dropped out of high school. He would babysit for his sister and would not go to school. Whenever I would tell him to go to school, he'd go out the front door and come back in the house through the rear door. None of my efforts were supported by his mother; she would not assist me in raising a responsible man. All Richard wanted to do was stay around the house and play games on television and watch cartoons. I knew that one day the time would come for him to face reality. That reality was being of age to work, and him not wanting to. I often have flashbacks about how abusive my father was with all 10 of us. However, all of us were raised to assume some kind of responsibility. Even my brother, Elbert, who didn't work steadily, drove a cab to earn a living.

Currently, Richard is working and making a law-abiding living. He has two jobs and is not home watching television or cartoons, and playing games. I am proud of Richard.

Lisa Mahone was my first biological daughter born to me and Grace. When Lisa was born, I was employed as a customs aide for the United States Treasury Department, Customs Service. She was born at St. Luke Presbyterian Hospital, in Chicago. Illinois. As a matter of fact, Grace was in labor for more than a day with Lisa. My heart went out to Grace for enduring such a hard labor during childbirth.

Lisa had the most beautiful brown eyes and light-brown, reddish hair. I never will forget how I had her sit on the chair while I worked at O'Hare International Airport. I took her around most of the law enforcement personnel whom I worked with when I was employed with the government. She met law enforcement personnel from the United States Customs Service, the FBI, Secret Service, the CIA, Chicago Police Department, Cook County Sheriff Department, and various other law enforcement agencies where I worked at that particular time.

Lisa was just like her father. She was hard working and diligent and I wanted to instill the value of work in her at an early age. I would give her tasks to do around the house and she'd perform them with any problem. As a matter of fact, Grace would not interfere most of the time. I knew then that my daughter would one day make some man a good wife. She would be a proud mother for her children, as well.

As time progressed, my daughter and I became very close. We were inseparable. After leaving the government, I took her around to the college teaching jobs that I performed. Yes, she told me on many occasions that she wanted to be like her father. However, there would be a strain in my relationship with her mother. That strain would leave my family as a somewhat dysfunctional one. Later, after Grace and I divorced, there was no male to lead the family unit. Lisa would go on and drop out of high school during her first year. She became abusive and promiscuous and started associating with the wrong crowd of peers. She also became pregnant. She became the child that I didn't nurture and raise to her teenage years.

My first daughter had a son at the age of 15. This is the time when other teenagers are playing in the halls at high school instead of nurturing a child. Oh my God, what a mess I have made. My father told me that it is not unusual for girls to have children at that early age. He said to me not to be mad. He told me to look up high and leave it in the hands of the Lord! My daughter had a baby by a drug dealer, who was a good father and supported the child. But as life would have it, he went to prison for five years for possession and distribution of marijuana. My daughter was left alone and she relocated and started going to college in Kentucky. She went to college to study criminal justice and is now a sheriff's deputy in Kentucky. Praise the Lord.

Angela R. Mahone was the third child born to the union of Mr. and Mrs. Melvin Mahone. She was born on January 30, 1978; and being the youngest child, Angela was spoiled rotten by her mother. She was sent to a private high school, while her peers all attended public institutions. I could not raise Angela the way that I wanted to raise her. My wife always interfered just as she had with Richard. I would give Angela a chore to do and she would ask her mother was it okay to do it. I knew that one day rearing Angela in this manner would cause problems.

Angela got pregnant in her senior year in high school, also by a drug pusher. She was 17 years old when she had her daughter, Briyanna Campbell. Briyanna is bright, quick to learn, and looks just like her father. She will probably in all likelihood be six feet tall.

I often asked my daughter if she planned to attend college. She would always skirt around the question. I was very unhappy and let down with her taste in men. I became tired of her going to work every morning while her boyfriend sat around not working. The only thing that I could hope for was that she would see from her own mistakes, rather than someone telling her. I also wished she find a decent guy. There are six percent of African-American males in this country. However, African-American males make up almost half of the prison population in America. Maybe that is the reason that she settled for less in her choice of a mate. At least, that is how I reasoned the situation. I pray that she sees her way out of the wilderness the way that her father did.

My Relationships

Due to my strict, conservative upbringing I didn't date any woman until I was 17 years old. I didn't engage in sexual activity until 18 years of age, while I was a member of the United States Marine Corps. From then on, I dated and married African-American women. My zodiac sign is Libra. My feelings are easily hurt. I have always tried to be fair and equitable in all the relationships that I was engaged in since the age of 17. Most women always took advantage of my kindness, honesty, faithfulness, and love. As a result, the relationships with these women did not end on a positive note. In fact, they failed. My first wife and I were married at the tender age of 18 years old. I was not ready for this marriage and she was not either. Her mother continuously interfered.

I finally ran out of steam during September 1980 and had to resign from the U.S. Department of Justice Bureau of Prisons for post-traumatic stress and depression. I would never be the same again. I was burnt out. My first wife never went out with me socially. We never went on a dinner date. Never went to church together. We never participated in any social activities outside the home. This lack of activity from being incompatible made me drift from my first marriage. My first wife did not go to college. She remained stagnate. We argued. We had domestic problems. Our sex life was not harmonious. We didn't know one another. She didn't understand me. I didn't understand her. We were apart more than we were together. We finally divorced after 15 years of marriage. We had three children together, the first was born out of wedlock.

My second wife and I were married for all the wrong reasons. We were married for lust. I had only known my first wife for three weeks when I married her in 1970. My second wife was an African-American beauty queen. I met and married her in 1986. She took advantage of me economically. She worked as a musician at church and cosmetologist and always found an excuse for *not* having any money. She would say, "I didn't earn any money today." She and I never went out socially; we never went to church; we never went to dinner. She was several years my junior. When I lost my job, she walked out on me. We were finally divorced after two years of marriage, in 1988.

My third wife and I were married in 1995. She was an accountant, and as with the previous wives, she did not file income tax together with me. She could never come to any agreement with me regarding saving checking, bills, finances. She was very private about her finances. I paid the bills. She never put any money in the house for finances. We never developed an enduring relationship. And like the other woman I was married to, we did not do anything together socially. We didn't even go to the movies. However, she did keep a clean house and she cooked well. Yet we were always in conflict with each other. She didn't get along with my daughters and they always clashed. And I did not get along with her mother. We were divorced after seven years of marriage.

As for my fourth wife, she was highly intelligent and had earned a master's degree in communications. She turned out to be an economic parasite. She always lied about her finances. I discovered she was very clever, unfair, and unfaithful. She was always insubordinate on her job and was late many times. She was terminated from her employment due to tardiness and absenteeism. She was unemployed for three years and I paid all the bills during this time. Sadly, we lost our house and we were divorced after being married for four years.

I am almost 60, and I'm looking for a lasting relationship. Hopefully, after learning from the past, I can have a lasting and meaningful relationship with a woman that will result in a life of marital fulfillness, happiness, and treasures for years to come.

The United States Marine Corps

I enlisted in the United States Marine Corps in May of 1969. The training was stringent and I was in several platoons while I was in boot camp. In boot camp, I was beaten by white marines on a daily basis and placed in a motivation platoon to motivate me. Because I was undersized, the drill instructor had me eat the leftover food from other marines' plates to gain weight. I finally graduated from boot camp in the fall of 1969. I successfully went through infantry and bituminous training before going home for Christmas that year.

In 1970, I received orders to go into combat in Vietnam. I arrived in Vietnam in January 1969, after graduating from staging training at Camp Pendleton. This training was meant to let the marine know what to do if he was captured and how to fight in rugged Vietnamese terrain.

When I arrived in An Hoa, Vietnam, at the end of January, it was during the monsoon season. I was assigned to Company "I" (India). The nickname for this company was Suicide India Company. After going on several patrols, I knew why the platoon was given that distinction. I met several marines who were on drugs because their significant others had written them rejection. In other words, their girlfriends and wives told them they would not wait for them to return home and they would find themselves someone to fill that void while these marines were in Vietnam.

As time progressed in Vietnam, I saw a lot of casualties. I saw some marines get their legs shot off. I saw brains shot out from their heads. I saw marines cry because their body parts were in such ill repair that they could no longer use their penis to have sex. One day, when I was at the hospital, a marine asked me, "Red, is my dick still in place?" I looked down between his legs, and told him yes, you still have a penis.

I would always have an epiphany when I was in Vietnam. I would have visions about the coming of the Lord and about different spirits. During my downtime, I would find the time to pray. I would ask Jesus Christ to not let any danger or ill will come down on me. Well, one day those prayers were answered. I was on a helicopter that was packed with commissioned officers. I was the only noncommissioned officer on the chopper. Our destination was Red Beach in Da Nang, Vietnam. My guess was that the officers were on their way to R & R, rest and recuperation, from combat. We were about 10 clicks out from An Hoa, Vietnam, when I heard hard thumps against the chopper. And then all of a sudden the chopper could not accelerate and gain altitude. It appeared that the chopper's hydraulic system was affected due to heavy gunfire that it had received. The chopper kept on getting direct gunfire hits. I heard screaming and yelling. The last thing that I remembered before I blacked out from shock was that an officer had dived on top of me to protect me from incoming rounds from the ground. When I blacked out for about 30 to 45 seconds, I had a life-after-death experience. I saw women angels with wings, hallows, and shiny white faces encircle me. They had smiles on their faces, as if to tell me that they were going to protect me during this crisis. I promised God during that moment that I would go to church if he saved my life. The angels opened the circle and smiled. I awakened. At the same time, the chopper leveled off and accelerated. The gunfire from the ground stopped. Apparently, the Vietcong was hit on the ground while our chopper was accelerating in speed at a low level off the ground and returning gunfire.

The reason that I was on that chopper to begin with was because I was on my way to the naval hospital in Da Nang, Vietnam. I had drunk water from a spring while on patrol and the doctors diagnosed me with enuresis. I could not stop urinating voluntarily. I was given a mild sedative and the doctors performed a procedure on me by putting a metal rod in my bladder. In the meantime, I saw an administration officer who determined that I was no use in serving in combat in Vietnam anymore. He offered an honorable discharge to me, and I accepted it. I was flown back to Camp Pendleton,

California, and given an honorable discharge on June 14, 1970. I was quite fortunate since there were many marines who did not return stateside. I did. I guess my prayers were answered.

Chapter

2

Stress in the Workplace

Authors Michael T. Matteson and John M. Ivancevich, in their book, *Managing Job Stress and Health: The Intelligent Person's Guide*, ask, "What can cause stress?"

A few immediate answers might be: problems with other people; performance pressures; overwork; boredom. The list is long, but the key factor is the stressful personality—yours, and, with relationship to work, your company's. You're a prime candidate for stress-related diseases if you're the well-known type A personality: impatient, intolerant, and strive for perfection and success. You can defeat stress by taking personal responsibility of your own problem.

The facts about good nutrition and common sense advice on such relaxation techniques as biofeedback and meditation can help you to limit stress in your life altogether, whether it is done as a long-term goal, to build the self-esteem crucial to a healthy personality, to modify type A behavior, or to know how to understand and manage whatever situation you find yourself in.

Michael T. Matteson and John M. Ivancevich both taught at the University of Houston. Matteson has researched and written extensively on stress, health, and job performance.

Ivancevich is the author of 13 books and many acclaimed articles on the relationship between stress, organizations, and heart disease.

Based on information covered in *Managing Job Stress and Health*, research states that in the last decade the only thing increasing at a faster rate than stress itself has been the public's interest in the subject. At such time, marital disharmony, deadline pressures, work overload, personal obsolescence, career stagnation, and a multitude of other personally disruptive conditions contribute to stressful situations.

We can take a cue from the character Edith Bunker (of TV's *All in the Family*), who once said in referring to her husband: "The trouble with Archie is, he don't know how to worry without getting upset." The trouble with many of us is that we don't know how to do a lot of things without getting upset. We get upset about traffic, about unreasonable bosses or incompetent coworkers, about having too much to do or having to little to do, about getting a promotion or about not getting it, the list is virtually endless.

Based upon the authors' research and experience, as well as the research and experience of others and myself included, the psychological climate of a workplace is predominantly determined by one's boss and to a lesser but still great extent by one's coworkers. In that light, each of us, whether a boss or a coworker, have a great responsibility for providing a decent, humane work environment—one that does not kill people.

Creating a stress-free work environment is not an easy task though. It requires the realization that we are working with other human beings. They are not simply coworkers or subordinates. They are individuals who need to be loved, recognized, and thanked. After all, some of them are literally giving their lives for the sake of the company or the boss.

Certainly, stress is a major concern and we will discuss it in some detail: what it is, what causes it, what it is not, what it does to you, and how you can control it. In a larger sense, however, this is a book about health: physical health, mental health, your determinant of happiness; and that stress—perhaps more so than any other single variable—can cheat you out of your happiness and possibly rob you of your life.

What is stress? Because stress means many different things to many different people, that is not an easy question to answer. Indeed, stress has been described as one of the most imprecise terms in the dictionary.

One way to define stress is to call it the force acting on you that causes you discomfort or strain. This is a stimulus definition of stress because it suggests that stress is the stimulus or force that acts on you, affecting you in some way. Some of you will no doubt recognize this as an engineering definition of stress, borrowed from the physical sciences. A dam, for example, will weaken and may be unable to withstand a temporary increase in pressure, which might occur when more than the usual amount of water is backed up behind it. Eventually, even without extra stress the dam will weaken to the point where it will collapse with little or no prior warning. In that sense, you are no different from the dam. If the stress acting on you exceeds your personal "elastic limits," you will weaken and collapse just as surely as a dam will.

Furthermore, stress, particularly as it relates to the workplace, is not:

- Being unsure of what the company (boss, subordinates, spouse, children) expects of me.
- Feeling like I'm not kept informed about what I need to know about my job.
- Not having enough time to get everything done.
- Being afraid of growing old.
- Knowing there is always someone else who thinks he (she) can do my job better.
- Commuting to work.
- Being afraid I won't get the promotion (I will get the promotion).

- Not being able to tell my wife (husband, closet friend) how I feel.
- Feeling guilty when I try to relax.
- Knowing there must be more to life, but not knowing what to do about it.
- Being responsible for other people.
- Living in the city.

Stress: Fact or Fiction Quiz

How much do you know about stress? Answer the following statements to test your knowledge:

1. People who feel stress are nervous to start with. True or False?
2. You always know when you're under stress. True or False?
3. Prolonged physical exercise will weaken your resistance to stress. True or False?
4. Stress is always bad. True or False?
5. Stress can cause unpleasant problems, but at least it can't kill you. True or False?

The correct answer for all five questions is: false. If you answered true to even one question, you're a victim of a stress myth. Another way of viewing stress is that it becomes the physiological or psychological response you make to an external event or condition called a stressor.

What else are you doing as you read this? Eating? Having a drink? Listening to the television news or to the stereo? Riding the subway or commuter train or van-pooling? If you are not doing anything else at all, you are probably part of a small minority. Today, most of us do not do just one thing at a time; we find ourselves with more to do in less time.

Alvin Toffler, in his popular book *Future Shock*, which examines the effects of industrial and technological changes, offers a dramatic perspective on the rate of change experienced in American society.

Change is easier to withstand if you have some feeling of stability or of permanence, but this has been taken away from many of us. While 50 years ago most people were born, grown up, worked, raised a family, and died in the same community, no longer is this true. Instead, today it seems as though the average American is born in one place, grows up in several different places, develops his or her career in a number of locations, get married, divorced, and remarried in still other locales, and ends up dying yet somewhere else.

Consequences of Stress

While some stress consequences, such as increased motivation and enhanced drive, may be positive, many are counterproductive, disruptive, and potentially dangerous. Below are examples of these latter consequences. Circle each one that applies to you occasionally; place a check by each one that applies frequently.

- Excessive daydreaming
- Anxiety
- Hostility
- Change in appetite
- Accident-proneness
- Apathy
- Forgetfulness
- Fatigue
- Irritability
- Stuttering

Stress Has Its Positive Side

It has been stated that stress is a response to our environment; in other words, it is brought about by change. If everything were totally stable, you would never have to change and never have to adapt. In fact, you would never have to do anything.

There is a type of stress that is a response to stimulation that you find challenging or satisfying. Without it, there would be no motivation and probably very little creativity. Thus, while many stressors result in distress, many may also produce eustress. Eustress is a term (from the Greek meaning good, as in euphoric) coined by Dr. Hans Selye, considered a pioneer of modern stress therapy; it refers to stress that is beneficial, curative, pleasant, and produces a positive stimulation. With eustress, you feel a sense of satisfaction, perhaps even exhilaration, in having accomplished a challenging goal. Overall, eustress is necessary in your life.

What Stress Is Not

In the book *The Stress of Life*, Hans Selye identifies several incorrect notions of what stress *is not*. They include:

1. Stress is not nervous tension. This is probably the most frequent misuse of the term, such as when we say "I'm feeling stressed about my upcoming performance review session with my boss."
2. Stress is not an emergency discharge of adrenalin. It is true that adrenalin production may increase under stress, but stress and adrenalin are not the same.
3. Stress is not always bad or always caused by a negative event. A promotion or a warm embrace can result in stress.
4. Stress is not always something to be avoided. Too little stress can be as counterproductive as too much.

Stress and Your Health: What You Don't Know Can Hurt You

Of all the possible consequences of stress, the physical health effects are perhaps the most challenging, controversial, and debilitating. Today, virtually no health authority would deny a link between stress and disease. Most current medical textbooks, for example, attribute from 50 to 70 percent of illnesses to stress-related origins. It is not a question of it does stress contribute to ill health, it is a question of how much and, in some instances, for long how does the effects last. The role stress plays in a person's health is significant; it contributes to disease and it does kill.

A Bad Day

We all have had what can be commonly described as "a bad day." Stop for a moment and think back to your last bad day. How bad was it? It might have been the occurrence of a single, major upsetting event: you did not get the raise you were expecting; you missed the deadline on a bid, perhaps costing your company a new contract; or your teenager wrecked the car. More than likely, however, it wasn't quite like that.

Rather than being a single major event, it was probably a series of relatively minor events, none of which was by itself is very important. More than likely, several of them occurring in a span of six to twelve hours accumulated and their effects caused your bad day. Imagine, if you will, the following sequence of events unfolding in your life on a particular day.

You awaken Monday morning at 7:15, having overslept by 45 minutes. "Damn it," you think to yourself, "Mondays are hectic enough at the office without starting off late." In your effort to hurry, you cut yourself in the bathroom while shaving and later painfully scald your tongue on too-hot coffee. While stopping at a service station, you fume over the fact that it seems as if the only time you ever need gas is when you're in a hurry. On the freeway, unable to change lanes because of traffic, you are caught behind a slow moving vehicle. Muttering under your breath, you unconsciously tense your entire body and tighten your grip on the wheel as you wait impatiently for an opportunity to cross into the next lane. Once you finally arrive at the office, you find dictation from the previous Friday still not transcribed and you chew out the typist without waiting for an explanation for the delay.

There are at least three aspects of this situation worth noting. First, you encountered a number of events that were potentially stress provoking: you overslept, you hurt yourself, and you were caught in traffic when you were already behind schedule; you found work undone that you had expected would be completed. Now add to that, you were embarrassed in front of coworkers, and you lost a credit card. And you argued with your spouse. These other events carrying stress-provoking potential may also have transpired during the day. The second important aspect of your day's experiences is that you probably transferred those potentially stressful occurrences into actual stress; in other words, because you were already stressed you introduced additional stressors into your environment that you might have otherwise might have handled more productively, reducing your stress and even eliminating some stressors.

The important thing to keep in mind is that an ongoing stream of relatively minor stressors, none of which by themselves is particularly harmful, can produce negative health outcomes even more unpleasant and of greater seriousness than those that grow out of single catastrophic events.

Duration of Stress Events

How long an event remains stressful is important and duration can be determined from the following categories:

- Short stress situations. This category includes the many usually mild stress situations that almost everyone faces daily.
- Moderate stress situations. These are events that last from several hours to a number of days. Examples are periods of work overload, new job responsibilities,

a continuing unresolved disagreement with a family member, and other events of moderate duration.
- Severe stress situations. These are chronic situations. They may last weeks, months, or even years. Examples include sustained reactions to the death of a loved one, protracted financial difficulties, prolonged physical illnesses, and inordinate and sustained demands in a work situation.

Maintaining Equilibrium

While we will make no attempt to present a detailed technical treatise of stress psychophysiology, we do feel it is important that you understand how the stress-health link operates. Likewise, in the stress-health relationship, the better you understand the process, the more likely you will be to make the proper diagnosis that, in turn, will lead to appropriate remedies.

When your environment changes, however, it falls upon your internal balance regulators to adjust. Such properties as body temperature, glucose levels, and blood pressure may be adjusted to respond to environmental changes. The relatively simple task of maintaining your proper internal body temperature in response to a change in external conditions sets off a sequence of events in your system that includes changes in respiration, cardiovascular functions, and endocrine gland activity.

Responding to a Stressor

The physiology of your body's response to stressors is really a description of how your body mobilizes in order to protect itself. Your stress response is quite extensive; the major body systems involved include your brain, the autonomic nervous system, and the endocrine system. The primary objective of these systems in a stress situation is to maintain or to restore the equilibrium that is threatened by the "invading" stressor.

Whenever you are exposed to a stressor, such as the imposition of a short deadline on a project for your boss or a run-in with a subordinate, the stressor is registered in your brain and "placed" in the cortex area. Your cortex in turn activates your hypothalamus. The hypothalamus is one your body's chief regulators; it is partially responsible for regulating emotions such as fear, rage, and euphoria, and it is also involved in the control of body temperature, appetite, and sexual behavior.

The most important set of glands activated by your endocrine system is the adrenals. Your adrenals produce the hormone adrenaline as well as a family of related hormones called corticoids. You can no doubt recall reading a news account of an accident in which a rescuer at the scene (frequently a parent) lifts a heavy object off someone who is pinned beneath it (frequently a child). In a "normal" situation, the parent would be totally incapable of lifting that great a weight. Numerous changes take place; some are noticeable to any observer, some are sensed only by you, and some take place without conscious awareness on your part. This complex pattern of events requires that significant amounts of energy be expended.

If you remain in a defensive posture for long periods of time, or for a long period repeatedly activate your defenses for shorter periods of time, serious negative consequences may result.

Other consequences of the stress response are recognizable as being counter to health and well-being. For example, the stress response elevates blood pressure. A chronic stress response may lead to chronic elevation in blood pressure. This is precisely why people with blood pressure problems are urged to avoid situations that may tend to upset them. Getting upset (stressed) compounds an already serious problem.

Disease Causation Formula

The relationship between chronic stress and other factors related to disease can be expressed by an equation used by many psychologists:

Disease= S x C x F, where:

S = an emotional stressor

C = your constitution or general state of health

F = other factors such as environmental conditions, medical history, etc.

This formula has three unknowns that help to explain why one person might develop a disease after appreciable exposure to a stressor whereas another person might remain healthy in the face of severe or prolonged stressor exposure.

Stress, Work, and Health

A useful, although somewhat arbitrary, distinction can be made between infections and chronic diseases. An infectious disease is one that is caused by a specific, identifiable (but possible unidentified) pathogen or microorganism. Polio, measles, and typhoid fever are three examples.

Negative health consequences of stress are probably experienced more frequently in the work world than anywhere else. This is due in part to the great amount of time spent in job- and career-related activities and in part to the combination of responsibilities accepted and effort put forth on the job.

Diseases of Adaptation

Ideally, your body adapts perfectly to every stressor it encounters. In reality, however, perfection is elusive and rarely achieved. In *Controlling Work Stress: Effective Human Resource and Management Strategies*, Matteson and Ivancevich point out "The degree of imperfection is frequently in such that illness is a by-product. The so-called diseases of adaptation are not the direct result of some external agent (such as an infection). Rather, they are the consequences of your body's imperfect attempt to meet the threat passed by one or more external agents."

The diseases of adaptation are sometimes referred to as postponable diseases. This conveys the fact that you can exercise a great deal of control over many of them if you elect to do so. Since they are brought about in large part because of your lifestyle, in many cases they can be postponed indefinitely by giving the proper attention to prevention. In the magazine *Science*, June Goodfield refers to these afflictions in an even more striking manner.

> Hypertension. This is called "the silent killer" because it is estimated that fewer than half the people suffering from it are even aware they have a problem. Hypertension is a blood vessel disease in which the blood flows through the arteries at elevated pressure levels. It afflicts one-third of the population over the age of 50. In most "well-developed" countries (including the United States), arteriosclerosis is an accumulation of cholesterol deposits in the blood vessels. As these deposits grow in both size and number, the affected arteries gradually narrow and lose their elasticity. This, in turn, greatly enhances the likelihood of a blood clot forming or of a vessel rupturing. If a clot forms a blockage in an artery that feeds the brain, the result is a condition known as a stroke. In this country, approximately 600,000 lives are lost to arteriosclerosis each year. The main cause of arteriosclerosis is incremental cholesterol build up.
>
> Ulcers. Known somewhat erroneously as the "executive of diseases," ulcers are inflammatory lesions in the lining of the stomach or intestine. They are directly caused by excessive secretions of the stomach across that attack the susceptible digestive system linings, causing irritation or

inflammation. High levels of corticoids are also thought to contribute to ulcer production. The manufacture of both stomach acid and corticoids is greatly increased during periods of stress. Thus, prolonged stress easily creates a perfect internal environment for the creation of lesions.

Diabetes. Diabetes is a serious disease, involving insulin deficiencies that render its victims unable to absorb enough blood sugar. Consequently, severe chemical imbalances may develop if nothing is done to control the imbalance; the brain may be affected, resulting in a diabetic coma. There appears to be little doubt that heredity plays a role in diabetes, possibly in the form of pancreatic deficiencies. Diet may also be implicated.

Headaches. These are frequently the result of muscular tension, the so-called "tension headache." Muscle tension is increased as you react to stressors, triggering the onset of a headache after a sustained period of stress. Frequently, the headache itself becomes a stressor leading to increases in muscle tension, which, in turn, increase the severity and duration of the headache.

Sexual Problems. This grouping includes impotence, frigidity, premature ejaculation, loss of sexual interest, premenstrual syndrome, and a host of other sex-related problems. Difficulties of this kind are complicated by the value our culture places on sexuality. Historically for men and increasingly for women, an active, satisfying sex life is associated with being a successful person.

Foremost among these is a reduction in the level of sex hormones produced during periods of stress. In males, testosterone levels sharply decrease during stress responses. Urine samples of soldiers in constant situations in Vietnam, for example, showed abnormally low levels of testosterone.

When these soldiers were taken out of combat, their testosterone levels returned to normal. There is evidence to suggest that sperm-cell production also declines during stress. In general, stress tends to diminish overall sexual functioning in the male, tending to make sexual activity unappealing and/or unsuccessful. Likewise, the amount of progesterone, the major female sex hormone, tends to diminish under conditions of stress.

Coronary Heart Disease (CHD): Heart disease is an epidemic. In 1980, more than one million people died from forms of cardiovascular disease, representing slightly one million Americans who have heart attacks and about 650,000 of them died.

Research on Stress, Disease, and Work

A great deal of research has been done on the relationship between stress, disease, and work. Examples of typical findings, all published in respected journals during the past 10 years include:

- Forty-five percent of a sample of coronary patients put in more than 60 hours a week on their jobs.
- Reported job stress was associated with high cholesterol levels, increased heart rate, and increased smoking.
- Blood pressure was higher among employees who reported that they did not completely understand what their superiors expected of them.
- Members of high stress occupations [Such as physicians and police officers] have suicide rates 2 to 6 times as high as that of the general population.
- Foremen experienced twice as many ulcers as did workers one level below and above them in the company.

Stress and Mental Health

Thus far, we have focused attention on the physical health consequences of stress. This is because, while most people today know that stress can make them anxious or depressed, not everyone knows the role stress may play in heart disease or diabetes.

Medical and occupational research abounds with studies suggesting relationships between mental health and job stressors. Mental health problems have been linked to lack of job satisfaction, work overload, deadline pressure, leadership style, job insecurity, underutilization of abilities, boredom, and repetition. With very few exceptions, most of this research is strongly supportive of an association between the presence of stressors in the work environment and mental health problems. Whether or not the outcome of stress is disease, it is clear that the consequences of stress are significant in terms of individual welfare, human happiness, and job performance.

How Stress Killed the Executive Monkey

Neuroscientist Joseph Brady reported one of the more compelling stress studies in *Scientific American* back in 1958. Brady's experiment went like this:

Two monkeys were strapped to a chair and given a mild but uncomfortable electric shock every 20 seconds. The "executive" monkey could avoid the shock by pushing a red button within the intervening period. If he did, the 20-second period would begin again. Thus, it was possible for the monkey to avoid all shocks if he stayed alert and made the correct decisions.

The only difference was that the companion monkey's button did not allow him to avoid the shock. Eventually, the executive monkey died, while the companion monkey remained healthy and even happy, except for the shock. You see, the comparison monkey did not have a stressful job.

To this end, this writer suffers from stress-related diseases such as nerve damage as a result of participating in combat in Vietnam, stress due to a long job history, and a recent successful removal of a defective aortic valve having had open-heart surgery in September 2009. I have had to change my life's habits and slow down. I have never smoked, drank hard liquor, or did illicit drugs. As such, I have been compelled to return to college to become owner/operator of my own motivational speaker's business regarding how to prepare for a stressful workplace milieu.

I will live a clean and healthy life. Thus, I have learned from the past to correct the future for my life ahead, in my community, and in our global market.

Stress and the Law Enforcement Officer in the Workplace

Developing mental health care to members of the law enforcement community is difficult. Police officers often resist counseling for several reasons. Frequently, they have a strong sense of self-sufficiency and insist that they can solve their own problems.

Counselors must have a thorough understanding of policing as well as a comprehensive knowledge of the police force and its demographics. They must be familiar with the organization of the police department and its power structure so they can understand the work environment of affected officers.

Because of their background and experience, some mental health professionals find it hard to understand who the law enforcement officer is and what is the occupation entails. For example, police officers often are seen as having a warped sense of humor, sometimes referred to as "gallows humor." Officers use humor to vent anger and frustration. Thus, outsiders of law enforcement might see it as sarcastic, callous, and insensitive.

When mental health professionals start to work with law enforcement officers, they soon discover that the officers evaluate them as much as they evaluate the officers. Often, the officer-patient might want to know about the counselor's familiarity with policing, their opinions of police officers, and their previous work with police personnel.

Some incidents in the careers of police officers leave a profound effect not only on the involved officers but also on their family members. Side effects of traumatic events might surface at home in the form of anger, depression, frustration, grief, insecurity, confusion, and disillusionment. Family members frequently become the convenient targets of officers' misplaced emotions.

Spouses might adopt the rules of either supporter or victim. As the children of officers who suffer from post-traumatic stress disorder mature, they also might exhibit the same fears, emotions, and cynical attitudes as their affected parent. As a result of working in every area of the criminal justice and having a PTSD condition from working in law enforcement, who would better counsel law enforcement officers than themselves. It is critical that law enforcement personnel counsel their own because they know what problems to look for when counseling law enforcement personnel. Mental health professionals should come from the ranks of their own.

M. Silva, "The Delivery of Mental Health Services to Law Enforcement Officers," *Critical Incidents in Policing*, eds. J. Reese, J. Horn, and C. Dunning rev. ed. (Washington, D.C.: U.S. Government Printing Office, 1991), 335-342

Chapter

3

Leadership in the Workplace

As the person who influenced this section of my book on leadership in the workplace, former New York City Mayor Rudolph W. Giuliani writes in his book *Leadership*, "Leadership does not simply happen. It can be taught, learned, developed."

As a child, my father led me. He was a role model I followed into adulthood. I didn't know how significant his leadership was in my life until I left home at the early age of 17 and volunteered for the United States Marine Corps. I didn't know how much I appreciated my father until the drill instructors gave me orders to follow. And I followed those orders. My father disciplined me when I didn't follow his orders. He was very conservative in the way he raised all of his children.

It was Supervisor Y in the United States Customs Service that gave me orders in the workplace. Supervisor Y just happened to have served 20 years in the Army. He was a lifer. He was a true leader in that he was a leader of men just like my father, as he raised me in the manner of the drill instructors in the Marine Corps. You see, leadership was demonstrated to me by these men in a very structured style from my adolescent years into adulthood. I was quite fortunate to these men with many years of experience in leadership training me.

I was 19 years old when I assumed a position with the United States Special Police, for the United States General Services Administration. This organization hired me because of my military combat record with the US Marines. At that time, I was the youngest police that they had hired. Many managers and supervisors in the General Services Administration and the Federal Protective Service had served in the military. Some of these men were lifers, the same as Supervisor Y had been, with the Army and in the United States Customs Service, Department of the Treasury.

Other personnel whom I came into contact with were also from military intelligence, the Federal Bureau of Investigation, Drug Enforcement Agency, Coast Guard Intelligence, Secret Service, and a multiplicity of other law enforcement agencies. I was fortunate to be surrounded by leaders of men who were well trained. Some had begun their training as university and college graduates, as well as having military training just as I had. These men were all leaders in the field of intelligence and law enforcement, and I felt privileged that the managers saw fit to hire me to work with them at such a young age. By interacting with these men, I had a firsthand look at how agencies were run in the federal government. Vicariously, I learned how to be a leader just by serving with them and being supervised by them as well.

A leader is a person who is willing to sacrifice his or herself by setting an example for others to follow and by managing others with their own unique style of management. They also work to meet organizational objectives in an efficient manner with their distinctive qualities and leadership style.

My first real boss was Gunnery Sergeant Rector, in the United States Marine Corps. He drilled me and taught me, and I learned and developed leadership skills from him. I was Gomer Pyle in the Marine Corps; and I others thought of me as naïve and a weakling. However, I was not. I thought

Gunnery Sergeant Rector was my enemy while I was in boot camp in the Marine Corps. He hit, beat, punched, drilled, and tortured me continuously. That's one way the Marine Corps shaped an unknown boy into a man. I scrubbed floors with a toothbrush; I exercised until I gasped for breath and mercy. I bled and I coughed up blood continuously. I screamed. I dived on concrete slab decks. I was beaten up by other marines. I cried. I marched in 98-degree heat for six miles a day on a regular basis. The United States Marine Corps Boot Camp was the most difficult training I have ever endured. After three boot camps and motivation platoons, Gunnery Sergeant Rector said: "You are the best recruit I have ever trained, I will fight with you anywhere in the world." Since he had to his credit five tours in Vietnam, I was honored. Gunnery Sergeant Rector groomed me for other training in the Marine Corps and to be a smart leader while in combat in Vietnam. I survived. The Marine Corps turned a skinny, underweight, ghetto boy into a confident man.

 I considered myself to be a leader. Thank God for the United States Marine Corps. God bless America. *Semper fi*, Always faithful! The rest is history in respect to my leadership abilities. I went on to marry; raise a family; work jobs with on the average of 13 hours a day contemporaneous to earning a B.S. in sociology, an M.S. in corrections, and a Ph.D. in criminal justice. I also earned enough semester hours for two additional master's degrees. As a result of my numerous experiences, as of this writing I plan to start my own business and teach as an assistant professor in criminal justice.

 Leadership, Giuliani writes, works both ways: "It is a privilege, but it carries responsibilities—from imposing a structure suitable to an organization's purpose, to forming a team of people who bring out the best in each other, to taking the right, unexpected risks. A leader must develop strong beliefs, articulate and act on those beliefs, and be held accountable for the results." These principles he illustrates with candor and courage throughout the pages of *Leadership*. He never knew that the qualities he describes would be put to the awful test of September 11, he says; but he never doubted that they would prevail.

Time magazine writes about Rudy Giuliani: "For having more faith in us than we had in ourselves, for being brave when required and rude where appropriate and tender without being trite, for not sleeping and not quitting and not shrinking from the pain all around him, Rudy Giuliani, Mayor of the World, is *Time*'s 2001 Person of the Year."

Leadership in the workplace is significant in today's business community. There are many definitions for leadership. My definition of leadership is a person who solves problems. One who is empathetic. One who takes charge and takes responsibility. One who sets an example for others to follow.

During my research, I focused on the writings of Peter Han. He is the author of *Nobodies to Somebodies*, in which he interviewed 100 leaders in business, politics, arts, science, and non-profits and talked about how they got started. I will discuss about some of these interviews with people who went from rags to riches, unknown to known. Han himself is a young Harvard graduate who cofounded his own software company and sold it in 2002. He has written for the *New York Times*, the *Boston Herald*, *Associated Press*, and magazines such as *Corporate Board and Marketing Management*.

In 2005, I was working in Bremerton, Washington, employed at Olympic College from 2005 until 2007 as the coordinator of the criminal justice department. This was before open-heart surgery changed my life even as of this writing. Han writes about professional happiness in his book. Happiness might be defined as doing something one loves, with excellence. As a person with type A personality, I am aggressive, hard driven, impatient, intolerant, and strive for perfection and success at almost any cost without fail. It is for this reason that I completed my Ph.D., worked long hours, was divorced several times, and raised three children alone with one marriage. I, in my past life, was a bureaucrat. I was an educator, law enforcement worker in every area of the criminal justice system. Today, I am a writer, administrator, manager, and a vanguard for new ideas to assist an ever-changing organizational workplace.

Han holds that leaders differ in how much freedom they had in taking their first jobs. For reasons of national service (as in times of war, with the military) or economic need, some people had more constrained sets of possibilities as they started their careers, while others had more flexibility and could do essentially whatever they wanted.

Research suggests that standards of class in society for leaders can make a difference for constrained or flexible possibilities when careers are assumed in the workplace. When I started my professional career after Vietnam, and being honorably discharged from the Marine Corps, I was poverty stricken in a fair economic job market. As time progressed, I gained professional workplace experience. Being employed with the federal government I was a bureaucrat. I was tenured. I was happy as a government worker. I was promoted due to my leadership abilities. I traveled to various parts of the world. I lived a rich life. I was skilled, educated, and intelligent. In short, I was and I still am a leader.

In his book, Han's subjects describe the numerous ways in which luck and fortunate circumstance had impacted their careers. Talent and passion also played a part in their achievements.

I see this as a rolling of the dice, as landing in an unplanned career can be due to fate and circumstance. John Sulston, an British winner of the Nobel Prize for physiology or medicine in 2002, explained, "Science is a random walk, and I guess most things that are worth doing are the same: the point is that the future is unpredictable, and should be approached with passion rather than career-minded worry." His experience was that passion, and his naturally pursed interests, shaped all that followed.

A continent away in a very different line of work, Senator Chuck Hagel of Nebraska described similar feelings. To him, "Life is to a certain extent about...the stream taking you, the currents grabbing you there are centrifugal forces that to a certain extent you have very little control over."

Hagel's knowledge of larger forces stemmed directly from personal experience. As a 23-three-year-old fresh out of college in his home state of Nebraska, he was motivated by a deep patriotism and volunteered to fight in Vietnam. Like his brother Tom, each led a squad of the US Army's 9th Infantry division into battle. Hagel emerged with two Purple Hearts for injuries received in fierce combat, injuries that easily could have extinguished his life before he got a chance to achieve his later successes in business and government.

As for myself, as an 18 year old from the West Side of Chicago and as marine infantryman, I, too, was motivated by a deep patriotism and volunteered to fight in Vietnam. I led and followed fellow marines into combat. I was shot down in a helicopter. I participated in ambushes. And I participated in various firefights. I served.

From the business side, Jay Gellert, the CEO of insurance giant Health Net, presented a similar picture in sharing how he took his first job after college with a small management-consulting firm.

"I'd done a little work with them during the time I was in college," Gellert said. "In most of my career, I've not really had a clear plan. It just seemed like a pretty natural thing to do...I don't think I really spent very much time thinking about alternatives." Han calls this "Random Walk." I agree to disagree; I call it passage over time due to one's constraint and flexibility based on their class and station in life mixed intermittently with each leadership role during ones career.

Wendy Kopp sets a good example of the conscious model for trailblazer. The founder and head of Teach for America, one of the country's best-known nonprofit organizations, reflects on the conundrum she faced as a senior at Princeton: "I suddenly realized that I was going to need to figure out what to do after I graduated. I went down to our career services center, and at the time the real options for liberal arts majors such as myself were graduate school and two-year corporate training programs. I began conducting a rather ineffective job search, half-heartedly applying to a few management-consulting firms, a few investment banks, a few brand management and real estate firms. One day, my search and my own passionate interest in education reform—and specifically in addressing the disparities that persist in educational opportunity along socioeconomic and racial lines—led me to think of an idea: Why doesn't this country have a national teacher corps that recruits outstanding recent college graduates of all academic majors as aggressively to teach in urban and rural communities as we were being recruited at the time to work on Wall Street? And I thought it would also ultimately influence the consciousness of the nation through influencing the perspective, career direction, and civic commitment of our nation's future leaders." Passion didn't produce immediate success, though. Kopp ran into roadblocks as she pushed to translate her idea into reality. And to blaze a new trail for her own career and others, she said, 'I wrote a passionate letter to the president of the United States suggesting that he create it as the 'Peace Corps of the '90s,' but my letter clearly fell in the wrong stack and I received a job rejection letter in return."

In a way, these mavericks might be considered the most stubborn of society's some bodies, the one least willing to fit themselves to existing rules and career paths.

Conversely, civic-minded trailblazers are conservative, transparent, and will stay focused on their goal in respect to whatever position desired. The more knowledgeable about their goal and their surroundings, their goal will be within reach. The trailblazer will passionately pursue an overall, focused career. Instead of a job. As a result of my overall background, life-threatening experience, I am focused, aware, and focused on a career instead of a place to work, a job. I am persistent.

Kopp, being well educated, skilled, having a burning desire to succeed, stayed focused toward her goal in life. She wanted to leave her imprints in education. Therefore, to this end, this writer began his thoughts on leadership by reflecting on the former Mayor Giuliani, who indicated that "leadership does not simply happen. It can be taught, learned, developed."

In respect to Han, *Nobodies to Somebodies* projects a multiplicity of traits on leadership in the workplace: intelligence, hard work, integrity, and perhaps a bit of luck. Han interviewed a roundup of leaders in the workplace to present the somebodies. These people often did the so-called right things in managing their careers: attend good schools, work toward responsibility, and persevered through difficulties with future aims toward their overall careers. The factor that separated them from others, and that propelled their rise from a nobody to a somebody, was the constant emphasis on understanding themselves, taking in environmental feedback and conditions, and working toward the rich new possibilities available in each given situation.

It is my firm belief that to be a successful leader in the workplace one has to be persistent; leadership is a reflection of person who is empathetic, responsible, and competitive in today's ever-expanding, ever-changing global market.

Capsule biographies of the leaders interviewed in *Nobodies to Somebodies* mentioned in this chapter:

John Sulston received the Nobel Prize in physiology or medicine in 2002. He attended Cambridge University and then later continued his studies in biology and genetics in the United States and Britain. With a team from Washington University, Sulston worked to sequence the genome of a particular species of worm. Sulston was honored with British knighthood for his services to genome research in 2001. He has a wife and two children.

Charles "Chuck" Hagel has been a US Senator since 1996. He was born and raised in Nebraska, then volunteered to fight in the Army infantry in 1967–1968, serving in Vietnam in 1968. He returned home to graduate from the University of

Nebraska in 1971. He moved to Washington, D.C., and held a variety of jobs in government before returning to Nebraska to work as an entrepreneur prior to his election to the US Senate.

Jay Gellert is president and CEO of Health Net, one of the country's largest managed health-care organizations. Before working at Health Net, he worked for a series of managed-care companies from 1985 to 1996. Gellert hold a B.A. from Stanford University and serves on several boards, including the American Association of Health Plans and Ventas.

Wendy Kopp is the president and founder of Teach for America. She created the organization in 1989, shortly after graduating from Princeton University. She has built the organization to more than 3,000 teachers and 7,500 alumni; she is one of the country's top social entrepreneurs recognized with a host of honorary doctorates from universities, awards from different organizations, and the Woodrow Wilson Award, the highest honor Princeton confers on its undergraduate alumni.

My Life as a Bureaucrat

Thank God for serving our country. With an honorable discharge, I was eligible for medical, housing, and education benefits. The State of Illinois paid an allowance for education, and I took full advantage of everything that I had going with the honorable discharge. I earned a bachelor's and master's degree from Chicago State University in 1975 and in 1977, in sociology and corrections. I was a federal protective officer (police), from 1971 until 1972. As a result of due diligence on the job as a police officer, while I was assigned to the United States Customs Service, I was noticed when I placed a ticket on the car of the district director of the United States Customs Service in Chicago, Illinois. He was illegally parked. While in that position, I made a suggestion about an unsafe pistol range, and my suggestion stopped injuries on the pistol range. Fragments from the bullet embankment put a number of law enforcement officers lives in danger. The suggestion was adopted. I was transferred to United States Customs Service in 1972, as an inspectional aide (import clerk). I was a GS-5 and my work included classifying and rating imported commodity. Due to excellent performance on that job, I was later promoted to customs aide (teller) at O'Hare International Airport as a GS-6/7, where my duties were to assess imported and personal commodity. Working for the United States Customs was exciting until I found out that they plans to promote me any further. I always thought if a person worked hard, he would be rewarded. That didn't happen. The management at O'Hare International Airport for the United States Customs Service did not want to promote me, I believe, because of my race. Personnel in management always told me that I was too smart for my own good; they told me that it didn't matter how many degrees I had, they were not going to promote me. Furthermore, they told me if I put in for 50 jobs and filed 50 Equal Employment Opportunity complaints, I would not receive a promotion.

Well, I began to look elsewhere for employment. What really aggravated me was the fact that people who did not have a degree would get a promotion. They boasted and gossiped about their promotions, and I could hear about their qualifications that didn't match mine. I had no choice but to look for work with another agency. I applied with the Bureau of Prisons, United States Department of Justice in Milan, Michigan.

The Bureau of Prisons notified me that they would hire me as a correctional officer and I would have to start as a GS-6. I lost a grade. But that was the only way to break the sad state of affairs that I was in at United States Customs Service. In 1977, I left US Customs and transferred to the Bureau of Prisons, United States Department of Justice. At the time, although I didn't realize it, I had jumped from the frying pan into the fire by transferring to the Bureau of Prisons. My first assignment was at the Federal Correctional Institution in Milan, Michigan. Here, there were a lot of redneck bigots.

And they did not try to hide their feelings about African-Americans either. Without me even telling them, the staff knew that I had a master's degree in corrections from Chicago State University upon my arrival to the prison in December of 1978.

One of my first assignments was to work the gun towers, where it was cold and the heater never worked. I froze my tail off. There was no need to complain about the tower. I was African-American and on probation and I had to pay my dues. In time, I started being assigned to other posts. The warden, however, told me that I could put my master's degree in my back pocket. In other words, I could kiss my ass with my degree. I was beginning to see that is was difficult for African-Americans to penetrate racism by working if they worked in a rural setting of corrections for the bureau.

I witnessed whites beating up African-Americans and could not do anything about what had transpired. When I did, I myself was injured. I believed a staff member kicked me on purpose when he found out that I had had enough of the African-American inmate bashings. I witnessed a white correctional officer placing marijuana in an inmate's sleeping bunk, yet I couldn't do anything about it without jeopardizing my own safety. This was an everyday occurrence. The white officers would always fabricate stories about the black staff to try to get them fired.

I stuck it out there it until it was time for correctional training in Atlanta, Georgia. In 1978, I came out first in a class of 30—for all employees to regardless of their title or status. I scored an average of 90 percent, even beating out medical physicians. All of the staff wondered where I received my education, where did I attend college. "Chicago State University, Chicago, Illinois," I proudly told them.

Upon my arrival back to FCI Milan, no one mentioned my achievements. They had heard about my score at the training academy, but no one congratulated me. At the same time, I was asking for a transfer to Metropolitan Correctional Center Chicago. Why? Because my wife was pregnant. When she finally delivered the baby, I was urgently needed back in Chicago because the baby was always sick. My infant daughter had bilateral pneumonia and was placed in an incubator. I would drive back and forth in the rain, snow, and inclement weather to see my wife and our third child. At first, the racist warden wanted me to quit and apply for the same position back in Chicago. He finally gave in and I was transferred to MCC Chicago in the fall of 1978.

At MCC Chicago, I found the staff to be more amenable and receptive. I was there due to my previous experience of working in an urban area; I was assigned to work most or all of the critical posts because I had federal correctional prison experience. I was lucky in that I had endured the racism and bigotry by my fellow correctional officers and managerial staff at FCI Milan.

At MCC Chicago, the warden, associate warden, captain, along with the other managerial staff were quite knowledgeable. I learned a great deal from all of the administrative personnel whom I was assigned to. They praised me for everything I did correctly; and when I did a task incorrectly, the administrative staff would take the time to show me the correct way in doing things. I never heard one racist remark. I couldn't ask for anything better than that at the time.

As time progressed, I was given duty stations to work that were critical to the institution. I worked the control room, administrative and disciplinary segregation. I worked the sixth floor, where the women were housed. I had the duty of escorting prisoners to the hospital when they were sick. One prisoner in particular, whom I took the hospital, stood out among the others. He was serving 150 years for murder from Statesville Penitentiary and was a known gang member of the Gangster Disciples. He was complaining of gas pains. I escorted him to the Cook County Jail without a weapon. There were no other law enforcement personnel to provide me any assistance or protection when I arrived at the hospital.

When we were in the hospital, I watched him and kept my hands in my pockets because I wanted to give the impression that I was armed, even though I really didn't have a weapon. He was handcuffed on his legs and wrists. We stayed at the hospital for approximately two hours, and I was glad when we left. Upon returning to the facility, I noticed that the prisoner was no longer in paint in pain. I couldn't figure it out. He had gas pains prior to going to the hospital and when we came back, within a matter of minutes, the gas pains had stopped.

As I made my daily security inspections around the prison, I noticed that the correctional facility had too many visiting rooms. I made a suggestion to the administrative staff that the numerous visiting rooms threatened the security and safety at the institution, and the extra rooms cost too much money to keep manned during visiting hours. I wanted to have one main visiting room instead of several.

The administrative staff took my proposal under consideration and soon adopted the suggestion. They reasoned that they needed to centralize the visiting rooms and provide one for segregation, one for the women, one main room for the rest of the institution, instead of having several rooms throughout the institution.

My suggestion saved MCC Chicago millions of dollars; and it was later recommended to other MCCs in the country as well. I was later promoted to correctional treatment specialist for my suggestion. Working as a correctional treatment specialist was very stressful. I did not have any experience using time management, and I worked long, tedious hours trying to get everything done. The secretary complained to the associate warden, and he tried his best to relieve me of some of the duties that were particular to the post.

As time went on, inmates started using staff to bring drugs into the institution. Rumors were spread that I was bringing in drugs to the inmates when in reality I was not. The FBI and DEA began an investigation regarding staff bringing in drugs into the institution. They trailed me to me girlfriend's house (I was legally separated from my wife) on the west side of Chicago. The area that my girlfriend lived was heavy with drugs, and it was belief that the FBI and DEA thought that I was bringing in drugs because of the association.

Over time, I got tired of being accused of doing things in which I wasn't involved, specifically with regards to drugs in the prison. I asked the warden if he knew anything about the accusations. He said, "No, Mel. I don't know anything about you bringing in drugs." However, it was my firm belief that the administration used me to take the heat off of whoever they were investigating while they looking into the main culprits.

I soon became burnt out, stressed out, and paranoid. I couldn't take the heat anymore. I kept on going to the warden with the same concern, and he kept on telling me the same story, "I don't know anything about you bringing in drugs into the institution." One day, I responded to a fight in the basement where food was prepared for the inmates. The person with a knife came at me and almost stabbed me. I made a 180 degree turn and left the area when I saw the knife come close to me. The inmate who tried to stab, or slash me, with the knife had permanent damage to the right side of his brain.

Later, I returned to the 19th floor and caught an inmate raping another inmate. The one inmate was much larger and muscular than the other inmate, and he had a razor blade to the smaller man's throat while he was raping him. I stopped the rape and had the rapist sent to disciplinary segregation. As for the knife incident, the associate warden said, "You know that you can sue." I indicated to him that I was not going to take legal action and that the FBI should be called in to investigate the incident. The administrative staff said that they would take that under advisement. As far as I know, the FBI never investigated the incident.

I finally got tired of the job at MCC Chicago and resigned in September 1980. I was labeled "paranoid, PTSD, and depressed" by the clinical staff. The government offered me disability retirement, but I did not want to admit that I suffered with PTSD and depression. In retrospect, I should have taken the retirement because I did suffer from those mental problems. I was in denial. I just did not want to admit that I had those problems due to all the pressure I was under in respect to the drug investigation and the attempt made on my life.

I had left the federal government position in 1980; and while I was at home watching TV one spring morning in 1981, I saw a bulletin on a local station report that an inmate who was serving a life sentence had escaped from two armed guards, disrobed them, and absconded with their weapons at the Cook County Hospital. Yes, it was the same inmate whom I had taken to the Cook County Hospital when I worked at the MCC Chicago. And he had used the same modus operandi, mo: gas pains.

My next station duty as a bureaucrat was the Florida Department of Corrections. I was assigned there as a probation and parole officer. Here, I was working in the deep South with a very intelligent staff supervising me. They were not racist in Miami, Florida. I had two supervisors, Evelyn Block and Tom Swenson.

Evelyn Block spent a lot of time training me and acquainting me with the everyday role of a probation and parole officer. She taught me how to investigate probationers' and parolees' backgrounds on a daily basis. She explained to me how to go to court and present a case for the state/prosecutor. She showed me how to do Pre-Sentence Investigations (PSIs). All and all, I learned how to be an investigator and write for the state. I had to conduct face-to-face interviews with the probationers and parolees. I had to go out into the community and do collateral interviews in the field. This was a fine job until a tragedy struck: Supervisory Probation and Parole Officer Tom Swenson was investigating a report that a parolee was harassing a female probation and parole officer. The parolee was on parole for killing a Florida State Trooper. To this day, I don't know to this day how this parolee was given parole by the state, but his parole was granted.

Apparently, he didn't like the way the investigation was going, or the fact that Officer Swenson was closing in on him by possibly bringing revocation charges in respect to his parole. Well, one night it happened; the parolee had fatally shot and killed Tom. The state quickly assumed an investigation into his death, and I took Tom's death very hard. I requested a transfer to a safe haven in the state. That place was Pensacola, Florida.

In Pensacola, an old situation re-emerged. There were a lot of rednecks and the racist attitudes and discrimination surfaced once again. On one occasion, an administrator told me that I would not get promoted for 15 years and that I had to wait my turn fro a promotion. In fear of losing my job, I simply said, "Okay." However, I didn't stay in Pensacola for too long because my daughter wanted me to come home to Chicago. She would cry perpetually every time that I phoned her from Pensacola. She would beg for me to come back home. Well, I finally got the nerve to leave Pensacola and the rednecks were elated. Why? Probably because they did not have to worry about promoting an African-American from the North.

Once returning to the Chicago, I assumed a position as a training specialist at Malcolm X College teaching in GED program. In 1985, during the same time I was teaching, I started working at the Bureau of Labor Statistics for the United States of Labor in Chicago. After a time on the job, I was given the worse area to supervise parolees—in Chicago Heights, in the far south suburbs. The male parolees tried to frame me several times by having their female family members come to the door in a negligee when I rang the bell at their homes or apartments. Well, the supervisor delivered on his promise to fire me after I was only on the job for three months.

In 1988, I was laid off from the position with the Chicago City Colleges, at Malcolm X College, due to low student enrollment. In 1989, I started receiving unemployment and Supplemental Security Income (SSI) because of my PTSD and depression. I became homeless. I stayed homeless for 1 year living at O'Hare Airport in Chicago, Illinois. Luckily, my ex-wife (We had since divorced) let me stay with her briefly in 1990. I gave her part of my $350 a month SSI disability check; I paid her $100 a month for rent.

After moving from my ex-wife's house, I lived in a homeless shelter for two years. The homeless shelter was the YMCA located at Chicago at Clark Streets. At the Union House in the YMCA, I became involved with study groups that were suffering from stress and other illnesses. and was being researched upon by psychologists from Northwestern Hospital and University. The medication they gave me had not helped my PTSD and depression, and I could not think for myself. This time came in my life came to be known later as the lost years.

The Lost Years

For a time, I felt as though I was lost in the wilderness and could not find my way out. I worked jobs that were beneath me. I even became an informant for the federal government by telling them about everything I saw on the streets. I believed I was being used for the good of everybody. FBI and DEA Government agents **contacted** me. We talked, taking long walks on the lakefront. I volunteered to inform on certain people and organizations, and the FBI even sent me applications to join the organizations connected with homeless support where I worked on a part-time basis without pay. I wrote more than 1,000 pages of information about stress, training, law enforcement, and protecting the president to the FBI; when they received the information, they said that I was crazy.

When I worked for a Democratic campaign, I remained homeless at the YMCA shelter because they were unable to find me employment. The Democrats did promise me work by telling me that if the aldermanic candidate won this seat then I would have a job in city hall. After the seat was won, I was not given employment. The alderman I helped to get elected in the 43rd Ward told me he owed his allegiance to his family and not to me, after winning the election. He did, however, give me $700 to relocate to California to stay with my sister. Shortly after I arrived in California, my family wanted me back in Chicago to help my ailing grandmother. I reluctantly returned.

In 1992, after living in the homeless shelter at the Union House in the downtown YMCA, I started working as a volunteer for the Republican Party. I supported President Bush. Again. I was used. I was put in commercials with the candidate, standing in the background, on a regular basis. I even joined the Presbyterian Church in Wilmette, Illinois. I did not have a mailing address; I was still homeless. I was not working. President Bush lost the election and Bill Clinton became president. This news apparently didn't sit well with the workers at the homeless shelters because all of them were Democrats and I was Republican. One night, I requested carfare to go to church in Wilmette, Illinois. I only received fare for one way. It was a message not to come back. To return, I had to walk from downtown Chicago all the way to church in Wilmette, Illinois.

To relive those moments, I can only say that I was living in the YMCA, Union House, homeless shelter, and volunteering for the Republicans in the 43rd Ward in Chicago, Illinois. I was labeled a Republican and identified by the employees of the homeless shelter. As an African-American Republican, I was told "Let the Republicans give you carfare to go to church for choir rehearsal, we are Democrats not Republicans."

My legs and feet were so cramped that I lost feelings in them. A motorist driving a Mercedes Benz picked me up while I was seen struggling to walk to church in Wilmette. I was determined to do good as a Republican and finally decided to stay in Wilmette with most of the people whom I had something in common with.

In 1994, I met two friends while I had a summer job in Wilmette. They were Todd Hansen and Dan Proft, two Republicans who helped me the most. As of this date, Dan is the only Republican who has gotten me employment. He will always be a friend.

Todd was a multimillionaire's stepson. He was running for state representative, and his district was to be the northern district that covered New Trier, Evanston, and other districts/suburbs in that immediate vicinity. Dan was to be his campaign manager. I was homeless and staying in the YMCA in Evanston. I volunteered for Todd and Dan. Todd lost to another Republican candidate. It was a bitter campaign. I stayed in Evanston and remained homeless when the election was over. Later, I volunteered for Governor Jim Edgar's reelection campaign in Evanston, Illinois. I was homeless, and fortunately I was allowed to stay in the campaign office. Governor Edgar won, but no job was realized for me. Frank Paul, the ward committeeman, would only find me mediocre employment as a sheriff deputy in Lake County, Illinois. That job was too dangerous and I did not want to carry a weapon anymore. After the election, Paul changed the locks and virtually put me out of the office.

The pastor at the church where I was doing menial labor let me spend the night at the church rectory for one night because. I was a Republican and he was a staunch Democrat from Chicago, and he even told me so as to the reason he would not find me housing. I found myself drifting toward downtown Chicago to Methodist Church. The pastor there paid my for a one-room homeless apartment for two weeks. He told me to go to Great Lakes where the military could find me housing. I did. At this time, I asked my sister if I could stay with her on the South Side for a while.

I will never forget the frigid, cold winters in Chicago. After staying with my sister for some time, my daughter Lisa allowed me to stay with her. I started work as a substitute school teacher and had to catch the bus from the South Side of Chicago to the southern suburbs to School District 149, to teach sixth through eighth grades. I had to change buses three times and then walk a mile to the school. Those were days that I will never forget. I suffered not having the luxury of a car to drive in the winter of 1995.

I started teaching criminal justice at Chicago State University in 1997. I also started working as an investigator and resident adviser for the Salvation Army Correctional Sanctions Center. Just when things seemed to be looking up, they went down. I had a severe stress attack in 1999 while working at these jobs. I was not on medication and had a relapse. I also lost my full-time job. I was at this time pursuing a Ph.D. at Union Institute and University. While I was in the hospital at Great Lakes, Illinois, the dean at the university sent a computer to my home in Chicago to do my coursework in criminal justice and corrections because of my illness. In 2000, I started working for Human Resources Institute, as a substance abuse counselor. This was a very depressing job and I resigned after working there for only several months.

Dan Proft, my political connection, helped to find me employment as an intake worker with the Department of Public Aid in 2000. I was forced to leave after a year because of budgetary restrictions with the state of Illinois. The governor laid off thousands of state employees, which indicated overspending and overbudgeting in the sum of billions of dollars. Dan, my friend, also found my wife Clara employment with the state of Illinois. She did not keep the job for long because of a conflict with her manager. I soon found her a job where I was working, at the Salvation Army Community Corrections Sanctions Center as a business manager. She was forced to resign from that position also due to a managerial conflict.

After leaving the state employment and the Chicago Board of Education, I returned to work as a substitute schoolteacher intermittently in outside school districts and as an adjunct criminal justice professor at several colleges and universities up to and after earning my Ph.D. in April 2002. I worked for Westwood College as an adjunct professor at various locations in 2004 until 2005. I interviewed for a position as one of their criminal justice coordinator in 2005 and was told outright that a white person would get the position. The person who was to get the job was an attorney, and I never did find out what his law enforcement background was, or if he even had any. I felt betrayed.

    I proceeded to apply all over the country for management and assistant professor positions in the area of criminal justice. I applied for approximately 35 positions in all and was selected for four of them. I choose a coordinator position of at Olympic College in Bremerton, Washington. At Olympic College, there was no minority representation like the numerous campuses where I worked since 1995. My plan was to work here as long as I felt I would get tenure. As it turned out, the tenure committee was not forthright. They started giving me problems at the beginning of the third year. They bought me out of my contract and I returned back to Chicago. Upon my return, I had to confront many of the same people whom I loathed academically and professionally. They harassed me and said, "Grass isn't greener on the other side is it." I found a teaching job at the River Oaks Campus in Calumet City, Illinois, and it was indicated that I would only get one or maybe two classes. The coordinator informed that people who had been at the college the longest would teach the most classes. I had a car note to pay and other expenses that were burdening me on a monthly basis. I called downtown at another Westwood College and found more work there. I also called another Westwood College at O'Hare Airport and got work there. Before it was said and done, I had eight classes. God blessed me.

    One day, I got lucky. I received a telephone call from a predominately African-American two-year college, Taylor Business Institute in Chicago. The president of the college and I hit it off positively the first time we met, during the initial interview. I felt good about this situation. For the first time in a long time, I felt I belonged. President Parker gave the okay to hire me as the dean of Criminal Justice and Security Administration. I started work on June 15, 2008. I had waited for a long time to work with African-Americans. Even though the college was struggling, I saw myself in a role that could help make a difference in the outcome of the college. I possessed a Ph.D. and I saw myself in my last job. Of course, I would do other things along with this position to earn money, but I was satisfied for the moment. At that time, I had applied to more than 20 Internet/online colleges and universities. I was to start working at Aspen University on September 1, 2008.

At Taylor Business Institute, I had the opportunity to use my skills. President Parker believed in me and appreciated my experiences; she told me of my worth as it was related to the mission and strategic plan for the college. I was promoted acting assistant dean of academic affairs after being at the college for two and half months.

Taylor Business Institute was the only private Black college in the state of Illinois that offered secretarial, business, and other advanced degrees. I was proud to serve in this newly appointed and pivotal role. In time, I gained knowledge holding the positions as the dean of criminal justice and security management and acting dean of academic affairs. President Parker had indicated to me that she would train me, and I have never seen a woman with so much knowledge about academics and administration.

Both President Parker and husband had been in business for more than three decades, and I had the utmost respect for both of them. They had seen hard times and good times. At Taylor, she had to make budget cuts and to make hard decisions when the time came for it; she had to do the things an administrator must do to make the organization viable, marketable, and cost effective.

I was proud to serve in the positions at Taylor. I wanted so much for the college to be a success. We were undertaking accreditation in study at the college. We were getting prepared for the Higher Learning Commission to evaluate our program. We had to pass this test because with HLC accreditation, our students could matriculate at campuses all over the state. They would also be better equipped to participate more so in the economic and employment market than they were doing.

Life at the Veterans Administration Hospital

The time I spent at the Veterans Hospital in Chicago and in Seattle nursed me back to life—mentally. Back in 1980, the Veterans Administration Hospital in Chicago indicated that I had a post-traumatic stress disorder (PTSD). During those days, however, doctors did not have the same medication to treat PTSD as they do today. At first, I had delusional feelings. I even hallucinated. 1 felt depressed. I had nightmares about Vietnam constantly. I did not think I would ever get better. Over time, I saw numerous psychologists and psychiatrists at the VA. My mental feelings went in cycles and sometimes I even felt psychologically numb. There were also side effects to taking the medications. I was often afraid. But I did not give up hope. I told myself that one day I would be a productive person again. I told myself that I would not let a group or team of psychologists and psychiatrists control my destiny. The psychiatrists told me that I would never work and be productive again. I told them that I would. They said to me over and over again, "Why do you keep trying to be productive, you are not mentally fit to do the same things that you use to do." I said that I was going back to work, and I would not let any mental illness keep me down.

I participated in PTSD study groups at the VA and saw see veterans from Vietnam who were in more dire straits than I was in at the time. Most of them were substance abuse users. As a matter of fact, when my psychologist found out that I was not a drug user, he would call me a World War II veteran instead of a Vietnam veteran, who was labeled as using drugs. In 1995, Dr. Dr. Peggy Chou, my psychiatrist for stress and depression, put me on corrective medication. Mentally, I was cured.

When I participated in psychological groups, I would try and talk some sense into various veterans about substance abuse. Many of them didn't listen. They had lost hope. The majority of them were not formally educated; they had not been employed for any continuous period; they not had been and were not productive in the workforce. These were Vietnam-mentality veterans. I had a lengthy and productive employment and education history, and I was not always in the condition they were in at that time. God knows I tried on a daily basis to talk to these veterans about not giving up on life and not using drug. But the majority of them only wanted to qualify for VA benefits. They wanted to drink and continue to use drugs for the rest of their lives.

The Seattle Hospital was ranked as one of the finest Veterans Hospitals in the country. I was diagnosed as having PTSD, high blood pressure, high cholesterol, and a tilted heart valve. I was fortunate that the doctors stated that an immediate operation on my heart was not necessary. They pointed out that with proper diet and care, there was no urgency with an operation. As for the PTSD and other problems, the doctors suggested I take medications for them until my situation improved. I was in the Seattle Veterans Hospital for more than a week with doctors running exams on me. I was quite lucky that they found the abnormalities to my heart in time. Although I didn't need an operation, I wasn't satisfied with their opinion and wanted a second medical opinion at the time. I guess I was paranoid, and I didn't trust anyone with my health.

I checked into the Washington State University Hospital, and the resident doctors there told me the same things as the doctors at the VA Hospital in Seattle. I wanted a better explanation of my medical findings from a private physician. And I got one. The doctors were very thorough and examined me from head to toe; and they came up with the same diagnosis that the VA doctors came up with. Nothing had changed. A doctor sketched my heart on a blackboard depicting my problem. She said that I had tightening of the muscles around my valve that led to my heart, and that's why I felt pain in my left arm around my shoulders and chest. She explained everything to me, step by step. I was relieved that it wasn't serious enough for an operation at that time. I felt very lucky. Intermittently, I felt pain in the left side of my body. I knew that the pain would eventually subside. I knew with the doctors on staff at either hospital, I would receive the medical assistance I needed to survive. I continued to pray that I would not have to undergo an operation. An operation would be serious at that time of my life. I returned to church and asked God for guidance about my medical condition. My pain subsided.

Medical and Mental Health

In 2007, I suffered a mild stroke and aortic stenosis; I had surgery in 2009. The operation was successful. I had a valve transplant. I have a pig valve, attached to my heart. I lost and gained more than 500 pounds since leaving the United States Department of Justice, Bureau of Prisons in 1980 due to post-traumatic stress disorder, depression, stroke, and aortic stenosis. I have endured numerous hospitalizations for PTSD and was told intermittently in the 1980s by professional mental health psychiatrists and psychologists that I would never be employed again due to psychological problems. It is now 2011, 30 years later, and I have earned a Ph.D. and have worked as a dean, coordinator, caseworker, substance abuse counselor, security guard, adjunct professor, probation and parole agent, parole agent investigator, mental health worker and social service worker. I am conservative; I am proud to be a centrist. I am proud to be an African-American living in America. I have overcome adversities. I have beat the odds. Why? Because I have leaned to beat the odds and have better quality of life. I changed my diet, I exercised on a daily basis, and I did not use illegal drugs or alcohol. I watched the hours that I worked during the week. And I did not undertake stressful employment.

Church and Youth

My journey with religious organizations was full of joy and laughter; it was good for me as well as with the young people and adults whom I came in touch with over the years.

It all started with my late father, the Reverend Elbert Mahone Sr. I loved my father and I miss him. He was strict and firm but fair. He was very religious. When I was chastised and given a beating, or as he called it, a switching, he would quote the Bible. We had a church in our apartment building and all the children went to church twice a week. My nieces, nephews, cousins, aunties, and uncles occasional visited the Straight Gate Spiritual Church at 1537 South Hamlin, in Chicago. The church was in the basement, and worshipping there was my first contact with other youth. I was a very naive adolescent and looked for spiritual guidance by my father. My mother would attend when she could take off from her business.

My father was extremely concerned about the youth because they represented the future. I became a role model for the other youths in the church. My father would pray from the pulpit to stop the violence on the streets in which young people were involved, not only on the West Side but in other areas of the city of Chicago as well. There was a gang situation on the West Side; the gang problem was so serious that several gang members were shot or killed on a daily basis. My father would try to get as many parents as possible, especially those with youngsters in their family, to join the church. There were so many families headed by women it was a shame. Where were the fathers at during this critical stage in the youngsters' lives? The odds were not on the side of the young people to finish high school or to stay crime free if he or she did not have the proper guidance from both parents.

We lived across the street from a youth center. The name of the center was called B.B.R., which was short for Better Boys Republic. This, at times, was a breeding place for the Vice Lords or the Cobras. The youth leaders would try to instill religion in the lives of these youths. As for my father, he would often feed some boys who were homeless and hungry and came by the house. He would say a prayer for peace. My father did everything he could to keep his children off the street by having them go to church and stay in the house. Whenever he would see me or any of my siblings, he would tell us to go home and do some necessary chores. He did not want us aimless on the streets of Chicago.

As time went on and I became an adult, I realized that as a result of the way in which I was raised and given the necessary religious guidance by my father, who was an ordained minister, I chose to work with the youth by volunteering on different committees. I became a tenor in the choir, which was the first committee I chose to work on with youths. I assisted the music director by putting the young members in the proper place so their voices would resonate better. I also was Sunday-school teacher. I learned to be a Sunday-school teacher by having been a substitute grade-school teacher. Here, I would read the gospel to the young people and have them get involved in the lesson of the word.

When I was homeless, I served on the homeless committee at the Methodist Church in downtown Chicago. I would assist the pastor in the food pantry and help the youths who needed shelter and food. There were a lot of wayward youths who did not want to go home because of parental brutality. I taught them how to use the youth hotline to call for assistance when they needed help from being abused. On the South Side of Chicago, 1 served on the Bible study committee, and assisted the elders with youths. These adolescents needed all the guidance they could get, even though many of were already juvenile delinquents.

When I served as a probation and parole officer, I would personally recommend youths who were under my tutelage to go to church for religious guidance. Some of the youngsters found themselves when they would go to church. I knew that going to church had helped me as a young boy, and I believed it could keep other kids from staying out of trouble and from joining gangs.

When I served as a probation and parole officer in Florida, I assisted youths who were on probation by having them attend a local church and get involved with the ministry. I can't tell you how relieved I was when many of them would come to me and say, "Officer Mahone, thanks for referring me to church, I found myself." If only other youths took advantage of the guidance the State of Florida Department of Corrections Ministry offered. The State of Florida Department of Corrections Ministry programs helped a lot of wayward youths. The youth ministry programs curbed recidivism, encouraged youths to stop using drugs, and referred them to better housing. The programs started the youngsters on the proper path to adulthood. Youngsters found significant and meaningful employment through the ministry while I was parole officer in Florida.

Youth Training Centers with the Illinois Department of Corrections

When I was employed with Human Resource Department Institute, I was assigned to numerous tasks as a substance abuse counselor. When I was assigned to St. Charles Youth Training Center for HRDI, I gave 12-step initiation speeches aimed to youths to stay off of drugs. I told the youths who were incarcerated to obey authority and not do drugs; I told them to stay in school and not drop out. The significance of staying in school would help them from returning to the center and it would also help them find meaningful employment in the community. I would tell them of the importance of becoming a law-abiding tax paying citizens; as a tax-paying citizen, they would take part in what all Americans do—they would become productive citizens in society by sharing their wealth. I would impart to all of the counseled youths to take care of their dependent children. By taking care of their children, they would not be dependent on the government to do so. When the government takes care of young adults, and their children while they are in training centers, taxes might be prone to go up for gas, food, utilities, clothes, national defense, federal taxes, local taxes, and other taxes that the government would affix a tax onto.

I would tell the young people to worship their own God. By worshipping their own God, they would pray for their family, and prayer would give them something to believe in as well. Prayer would give them hope. Prayer would make them believe in the Lord. I would tell them not to deny that they had a drug problem. If they find themselves going back to anyplace that they frequented prior to being incarcerated, they would relapse. And relapse means a lot of substance-abuse counseling to youths.

Let's take the average youth whom I counseled at St. Charles Youth Correction Institution. The average young person feels that if he did not use drugs, he would not relapse. He did not realize that even though he did not use drugs, he would still be in denial if he frequented with people, went to places, and did things that he was involved in the community before he came to the correctional facility. I had to convince the youths that they should not deny being involved with drugs or their surroundings. By denying their drug usage, he would still be addicted, and it would difficult overcome substance abuse. It was very important that they followed my instructions when it came to denial and admitting their substance abuse.

Once they were released from incarceration, the most important step came into play. The most important play was "aftercare." Aftercare was significant because in reality this was when rehabilitation began. Their "freedom" would be tested.

As a substance-abuse counselor for HRDI, I was charged with planning, organizing, directing, controlling, and coordinating substance abuse groups once parolees and probationers were released from the jurisdiction of prisons and the court. Although these residents were technically still within the jurisdiction of the county, court, or the state, they had to attend drug-counseling classes several times a week and they had to give urine samples to satisfy the orders of their probation or parole. It was always my sentiment that rehabilitation began at this crucial time because this is when the probationer or parolee was put to the test to really find out if he or she wanted to become rehabilitated or not relapse and return to prison. When a parolee is in prison, he will do anything to free himself from custody. He will lie to authorities about being rehabilitated and not use drugs when he is released from custody goes to back into society and to his freedom. He will lie about committing drug crimes to support his habit. You see, when a parolee is in prison he will do whatever is necessary to see the light of day. The light of day is "freedom."

I learned this was the case when I was a corrections officer, correctional treatment specialist, and a resident adviser.

When I worked under the auspices of the US Department of Justice, Bureau of Prisons, I learned that young males who were up for parole would learn the "game" as to how to beat the system, and get paroled. They would join the chaplaincy, youth choir, Bible study, counseling sessions, and substance-abuse sessions to have enough points to be released from prison, jail, or the training center. That's why I would always say that internal programming was not the real test to rehabilitate, but the real test to rehabilitate would be external programs when a parolee or probationer was released from the designated authorities into aftercare for treatment.

Programming skills such as with computers and electronics prepared an inmate for meaningful and gainful employment. Other trades such as barbering and auto mechanics, which also falls under this category, can help the parolee overcome substance abuse as well. However, even when these trades were used, the youngster who is a parolee or probationer would still have to be serious about saying no to drugs and taking advantage of worthwhile programs to beat a habit.

Probably the worse situation for a probationer or parolee to become involved in would be to be released from an institution and relocate to the same living environment that he or she came from. They return to all the negative, drug laden, and criminal elements they left and only to find themselves a part of it again. In some instances, it seems as though the authorities and the system only set them up to fail. It is the system's fault and the system has the audacity to blame it on the recidivists when we have failed by offering improper programming when placing them back into their community. It is time that penologists wake up and say to ourselves, "Stop, look, and listen" as to how we are committing crimes ourselves by making it easier for criminals to relapse and to participate in a continuing criminal enterprise of the mind.

Education and Youth

Education is a lifelong learning experience. Learning is an enduring change of behavior. As a child, my father would always tell me, "Son, you are the sixth child of ten, you will need more education than any of the ten." Well, my father was correct. I did need more education than the other children. I hit hard times economically. I have been homeless. I have been grossly discriminated against by the government and other employers. It is my belief that my father had enough foresight to see that I needed that extra push to survive.

I was lucky compared to most youths when it came to academics. There was a Jewish teacher, Mr. Ackerman who took me under his wings when I was in the fifth grade. He always would say, "Mahone, don't eat greasy spoon food." He always took the needed, extra time to teach African-Americans. He was one of the few Jewish teachers in the school. The William Penn School covered grades through sixth. As a child, I was the victim of being bullied most of the time because of my slender build and quiet personality. Most of the older and younger boys knew that my father was a minister and that he had his church in our basement where we resided.

I was often the victim of mockery more times than not by children whom I went to school with from time to time.

My favorite subjects in school were social studies and civics. I would never really study for these two subjects, yet, more so than not, I'd receive As for these subjects. Math was the most difficult subject. There was a teacher by the name of Mr. Rivers, who was from the South, who would have you use a pointer at the blackboard to solve fractions and other math problems. There was one problem: If you incorrectly did the problem after he had gone over the problem several times, he would hit you hard with the pointer. Back in the early 1960s, if you complained to your mother or father at home, they would also give you a hit. And when you received a beating in those days it was brutal. Teachers were aware of that, and that is why they took full advantage of the moment and time to use corporal punishment. It goes without saying that if one gets an education then he or she can expect to earn more than the person who did not get as much education. My father would always tell me, "Son, I worked hard enough for all ten of you all." My father only had two years of grade school. He was very good with his hands and worked in a steel cutting company for 25 years. Even though, he was never late and was more productive than the average coil worker, my father's highest paycheck was $100.00 per week. This was between 1950 and 1975. I watched my father go to work in the rain, sleet, and snow. He kept on working because he knew that he had to feed 10 children. He has always been an inspiration to me. Though he only had a second grade education, he knew the value of getting an education. God, what a man. He will always serve as a religious role model and education inspiration for me for years to come.

What we need in our community are more strong educational organizations. Madeleine Albright, former US Secretary of State, indicated, "Breakthrough is based on what I believe is exactly the right formula—the community helping individuals to reach beyond their potential thereby enabling those individuals to enrich the community." Breakthrough Collaborative is a national nonprofit that increases educational opportunity for high-potential, low-income, middle-school students and inspires outstanding college and high-school students to pursue careers in education. Consistently featured as a Top 10 Internship by *The Princeton Review*, Breakthrough's innovative Students Teaching Students model partners middle-school students with college and high-school students who serve as teachers, role models and mentors, providing real-life examples that it's cool to be smart.

Based on data from the organization's Web site, Breakthrough boasts a proven ripple effect of positive results: 82 percent of breakthrough student alumni are accepted to college preparatory programs and 72 percent of Breakthrough teachers, many of whom were Breakthrough students, go on to pursue professional careers in education.

Drawn from the public school system, 89 percent of Breakthrough's students are students of color and 65 percent qualify for free or reduced-price lunch programs. English is a second language for 27 percent of its students, and most will be the first in their family to attend college.

Students commit to a minimum of two years of tuition-free intensive six-week summer sessions and after-school programs in which they take classes in core academic subjects, and participate in elective courses ranging from astronomy to African-American literature. Breakthrough's classes are rigorous and small (a maximum 4:1 student to teacher ratio) and full participation is expected of every student. Breakthrough was founded in San Francisco in 1978 as "Summerbridge" and serves more than 2,500 middle-school students and trains 700 college and high school students in 34 Breakthrough sites across the US and in Hong Kong.[1]

"I like to use 'breakthrough' as a noun to reflect the breakthroughs that take place when students teach students, or when a child becomes the first in her family to go to college or when a fabulous college student realizes that he wants to teach as a career," said Jessica D'Arcy, founding director, Breakthrough Austin. "Breakthrough captures the joy of learning—those a-ha moments when the light switches on and things that seemed too difficult or out of reach are suddenly possible."

Abstinence and Youth

My mother and father had five girls born to them within wedlock. They taught all five of them *not* to have sex with any boy until they were married. That was the conservatism they projected to the family. They also taught the five boys the very same thing, over and over again. As a result, none of the Mahone siblings had children born out of wedlock. Whenever one of my sister's would go out on a date, they had a curfew. They had to be in the house by 10 p.m.

I vividly recall my sister Betty Jean not keeping to the curfew when she went on her prom. My father scolded her and hit her for not keeping up with the curfew. The curfew was every night, and it was set even for special occasions.

I always preached "You are what you preach." My father was a disciplinarian. I tried to be one like him, but my wife and I separated and divorced after 15 years of marriage, making it challenging to raise our children. When my eldest daughter, Lisa, became pregnant at the tender age of 14, I will never forget what my father told me as we were walking back from my grandmother's house on Harding Avenue. He said, "Son, nowadays, it is common for young girls to have babies, don't be mad or angry at your daughter." I never forgot those words my father said to me that hot, summer day. I always looked up to my father. He would always give me words of wisdom, just like my mother and grandmother would during a time of crisis.

I was going through a transition in life myself. I was separated from my wife Grace, who had three children with me. She was the only woman whom I had children with; I never had any other children. That was important to me. I only wanted my children to belong to one spouse. I got a vasectomy at the age of 28. I had sex with other women being separated and divorced. I was always told that when you are grown, you have other options. You can make a multiplicity of choices. I did not want to procreate without being married. I did not want to bring shame and dishonor to my children by having children by another women without being married to her. If the woman had children when I went into the marriage that would be different.

The Bible tells us that we are not suppose to have sex unless we are married and for the purpose of procreating. God, I have sinned. God, please forgive me. I have had numerous girlfriends whom I will speak about later. I had sex outside of wedlock with all of them. It is for this reason that I can speak to the youths I give advice to from a religious point of view. This is one point of view. However, what about diseases? In New York alone, 25 percent of the people tested in some areas are HIV positive.

Ideas about sex and family occur in progressive stages in life. The first stage for a young girl is doll play. You see, doll play is supposed to teach a girl what a baby is, as the little girls is introduced to family culture and notions about maternal nurturing. During this time, the girl will play with the doll. The girl will feed the baby; comb the doll's hair; wash the baby-doll clothes. The doll will stand in as the baby that the young girl hopes to have when she becomes an adult.

Next are the adolescent and teenage years. The girl will move into move into puberty, which often means that she is capable of having a baby and she will have a monthly period. When this happens, she usually asks for permission to have a boyfriend and to be accompanied to parties, movies, church, sweet sixteen parties, etc. She will have nice clean fun. She will even start taking sex education classes in school.

She will be instructed not to have sex; she will be taught not to have sex even with a protection. When a teenager starts having sex, it's usually because of peer pressure or because of other reasons, such as dysfunctional relationships at home.

When I teach teenage girls and give them motivational speeches, I tell them to say "no" to sex. They immediately ask me, "suppose we use a condom?" I immediately say, "You are still having sex and the condom can slip off. You can get pregnant. You can catch a disease. And the ultimate could happen, you can get HIV." These teenage girls have not come of age as yet. While they are still under the guidance of their mother and father, most of them are latchkey children. Some of them do not have continuous proper supervision. For many of them, their moms are working moms due to economics in America. The family is a matriarchal-headed household. In some cases, the mother is the sole breadwinner. Not the father. And it takes both parents to be employed and to provide for their household. When I spoke with teenage girls in social services, they would tell me no one was home to supervise them and they had a lot of free time on their hands.

The other extreme is when the mother or father is incarcerated and an uncle, an aunt, or a grandmother rears the child. This is a usual occurrence these days, partly for reasons that include an unstable economy, uneven educational system, the War on Drugs, and the War on Crime. In far too many instances, this is a common situation yet it paints a bleak picture for young mothers, young fathers, and their children.

Leadership of the Family by My Father

As a child, I remember my father being an authoritative leader. As a matter of fact, during my adolescent years, my father managed the family with a strong hand, and in a way that we knew who was the boss, and who we were to report to on a regular basis for the everyday decisions regarding family matters. In the past decades, management experts have undergone a revolution in how to define leadership roles and what their attitudes were toward it.

We, as a society, over the years, have seen the classical autocratic approach change to a participative way of being led and managed. Different styles were needed for different situations, and each leader needed to know when to exhibit a particular approach of leadership to their subordinates.

My father used his leadership style with our family in order to get us to accept him and to follow him no matter what the issue at hand might have been at that particular time. My father's leadership approach was defined this way: When one can get his or her subordinates to accept and follow their prerogatives without their subordinates not challenging them, but following them in whatever their endeavors were at that particular time.

There is also a clear division between the leaders and the followers. Authoritarian leaders make decisions independently, with little or no input from the group. Some family members lacked ambition, disliked responsibility, and were docile. They wanted to be led. I was a child, I wanted and desired to be led. Children are often very easy to be led, and therefore do not lead. They are led by their superiors in the family.

The other form of leadership my father demonstrated surfaced when he knew firsthand how we were going to react to his leadership role toward us as a family unit. Therefore, he did not have to rule with an iron-clad fist. That leadership approach was laissez-faire leadership. With this, my father minimally got involved in decision-making and encouraged family members to make their own decisions.

The exact origins of the term laissez-faire as a slogan of economic liberalism are uncertain. According to historical folklore and research, the phrase stems from a meeting in 1680 between the powerful French Finance Minister Jean-Baptist Colbert and a group of French businessman led by a certain M. Legendre. The definition: "leave us alone," "let us do," "allow to do." My father laid down the foundation for us to be led. Therefore, laissez-faire leadership was appropriate in our family for us to be led. It may seem odd, but laissez-faire leaders are minimally involved in decision-making.

PTSD and Community-Based Corrections

When I was employed at the Salvation Army Community Corrections Center, located at 105 South Ashland in Chicago, Illinois, I was stressed out. I was forced to resign under the same modus operandi as the Federal Bureau of Prisons back in 1980. Historically, the Federal Bureau of Prisons had the Salvation Army Community Corrections Center under a federal work contract. It was the largest community correctional center in the United States.

I was working more than 13 hours per day in the center. I was working on my Ph.D. at Union Institute and University in Cincinnati, Ohio, in 1999. I was also working on an internship for my Ph.D. in the Cook County Public Defenders Office, in Chicago. I was an intern in drug court working four hours per night.

At the time, I was taking the wrong medication. The medication was not strong enough to control my PTSD condition and I was extremely burnt out and paranoid. The equipment that I used would not work and management would not repair the equipment either. I was working long hours to get all the work done at the center and management would not cooperate with me.

Stress and the Law Enforcement Officer

Perhaps the most insidious and least visible of all threats facing law enforcement personnel today is debilitating stress. While some degree of stress can be a positive motivator, serious stress, over long periods of time, is generally regarded as destructive, even life threatening. For example, police officers who worked around the clock in 1994 searching for two missing South Carolina boys whose mother first reported them as kidnapped found the case especially stressful since it brought to mind many emotions. "I feel like I aged ten years in ten days," said Union County Sheriff Howard Wells, after Susan Smith confessed to murdering their sons. [2]

Research further suggests that stress is a natural component of police work. [3] The American Institute of Stress, based in Yonkers, New York, ranks police among the Top 10 stress-producing jobs in the country. [4] Danger, frustration, paperwork, the daily demands of the job, and a lack of understanding from family members and friends contribute to the negative stress that officers experience. The Bureau of Justice Statistics points out that "exposure to violence, suffering, and death is inherent to the profession of the law enforcement officer. There are other sources of stress as well. Officers who deal with offenders on a daily basis may perceive the public's opinion of police performance to be unfavorable; they often are required to work mandatory, rotating shifts; and they may not have enough time to spend with their families. Police officers also face unusual, often highly disturbing, situations, such as dealing with a child homicide victim or the survivors of vehicle crashes." [5]

Some of the stressors in police work are particularly destructive. One is frustration brought on by the inability to be effective, regardless of the amount of personal effort expended. From the point of view of the individual officer, the police mandate is to bring about some change in society for the better. The crux of police work involves making arrests based on thorough investigations that lead to convictions and the removal of offenders from society—all under the umbrella of the criminal law. Unfortunately, reality is often far from the ideal. Arrests may not lead to convictions. Evidence available to the officer may not be allowed in court. Sentences imposed may seem to "light" to the arresting officer. The feeling of powerlessness and frustration that come from seeing repeat offenders back on the streets and from witnessing numerous injustices worked on seemingly innocent victims may greatly stress police officers and cause them to question the purpose of their professional lives. It may also lead to desperate attempts to find relief. As one researcher observes, "The suicide rate of police officers is more than twice that of the general population...."[6]

Another source of stress—that is of living with constant danger—is incomprehensible to most of us. Even to the family members of many officers. As one officer says, "I kick in a door and I've have to talk some guy into putting the gun down And I go home, and my wife's upset because the lawn is not cut and the kids have been bad. Now, to her that's a real problem.[7]

Stress is not unique to the police profession, but because of the "macho" attitude that has traditionally been associated with police work, denial of the stress may be found more often among police officers than in other occupational groups. Certain types of individuals are probably more susceptible to the negative effects of stress than are others. The type

A personality, popularized 30 years ago, is most likely to perceive life in terms of pressure and performance. Type B people are more laid back and less likely to suffer from the negative effects of stress. Police ranks, drawn as they are from the general population, are filled with both stress-sensitive and stress-resistant personalities.

Stress Reduction

It is natural to try to reduce and control stress.[8] Humor helps, even if it's somewhat cynical. Health-care professionals, for example, are noted for their ability to joke around patients who are seriously ill or even dying. Police officers may similarly use humor to defuse their reactions to dark or threatening situations. Keeping an emotional distance from stressful events is another way of coping with them, although such distance is not always easy to maintain. Police officers who have had to deal with serious cases of child abuse have often reported on the emotional turmoil they experienced as a consequence of what they saw.

The support of family and friends can be crucial in developing other strategies for handling stress. Exercise, meditation, abdominal breathing, biofeedback, self-hypnosis, guided imaging, induced relaxation, subliminal conditioning, music, prayer, and diet have all been cited as useful techniques for stress reduction. Devices to measure stress levels are available in the form of handheld heart-rate monitors, blood pressure devices, "biodots" (which change color according to the amount of blood flow in the extremities), and psychological inventories.

A new approach to dealing with stress among police officers holds that the amount of stress an officer experiences is directly related to his or her reactions to potentially stressful situations.[9] Officers can filter out extraneous stimuli and those who can distinguish between truly threatening situations and those that are benign are much less likely to report job-related stressors than those lacking these abilities. Because stress-filtering abilities are often closely linked to innate personality characteristics, some researchers suggest careful psychological screening of police applicants to better identify those who have a natural ability to cope with situations might perceive as stressful.[10]

The family members of police officers often report feelings of stress that are directly related to the officer's work. The Bureau of Justice Statistics has identified six sources of family stress: (1) shift work and overtime, (2) concern over the officer's inability or unwillingness to express feelings at home, (3) fear that the spouse will be killed in the line of duty, (4) presence of a gun in the home, (5) the officer's 24 hour role as a law enforcer, and (6) avoidance, teasing, or harassment of the officer's children by other children because of the parent's job.[11] In recent years, police departments nationwide have begun to realize that family problems and stress can negatively affect the quality of a police officer's work and the overall performance in the department. As a result, some departments have developed innovative programs to allay family stress. The Collier County (Florida) Sheriff's Office Spousal Academy, for example, is a family support program that offers training to spouses and other domestic partners of deputies and recruits who are enrolled in the department's training academy. The 10-hour program deals directly with issues that are likely to produce stress and informs participants of department and community resources that are available to help them. Peer support programs for spouses and life partners and for adolescent children of officers are also beginning to operate nationwide.

Officer Fatigue

Like stress, fatigue can affect a police officer's performance. As former police officer and criminologist Bryan Vila points out in his book *Tired Cops: The Importance of Managing Police Fatigue*, "Tired, urban street cops are a national icon. Weary from overtime assignments, shift work, night school, endless hours spent waiting to testify, and the emotional and physical demands of the job, not to mention trying to patch together a family and social life during irregular islands of off-duty time, they fend off fatigue with coffee and hard bitten humor."[12] Vila found levels of police fatigue to be six times as high as those of shift workers in industrial and mining jobs.[13] As Vila notes, few departments set work hour standards, and fatigue associated with the pattern and length of work hours may be expected to contribute to police accidents, injuries, and misconduct.

To address the problem, Vila recommends that police departments "review the policies, procedures, and practices that affect shift scheduling and rotation, overtime moonlighting, the number of consecutive work hours allowed, and the way in which the department deals with overly tired employees."[13] Vila also suggests controlling the work hours of police officers, "just as we control the working hours of many other occupational groups."[14]

Research by the FBI suggests that organizational stressors, such as inadequate training, poor suspension, lack of recognition for superior service and performance, perceived nepotism for promotions and financial incentives, inadequate pay, and insensitivity to personal needs, often cause discord. Job stress, such as long hours, on-call extended periods outside home, can cause undue and irreversible stress. Many law enforcement officers have personal problems just like everyone else. Naturally, affects to all of the body's systems, muscle, bone, cardiovascular, respiratory, nervous system, immune system, and neuroendocrine have strong consequences. Eventually, fading acuity, failing hearing, memory loss, diminishing muscle mass, dwindling dexterity, and attenuating balance impose limitations on officers with experience alone cannot always offset according to the FBI report on stress, depression, and paranoia. Also, suicide is common when a person has been under stress as well, as it happened to me. Critical incidents of stress leave some officers with acute stress disorder (ASD) or (PTSD) and many more with transitory symptoms, intrusive thoughts, sleeping difficulties, changed eating habits and patterns of emotional responses, the report said.

Me and My God

When I was going through my trials and tribulations, it took faith and the trust in God to overcome all the adversities that I was going through from 1969 until the present. I thought about a biblical character Job. Job is a character in the Book of Job in the Hebrew Bible, as well as a prophet in Islam. In brief, the book begins with an introduction to Job's character—he is described as a blessed man who lives righteously. Satan, however, challenges Job's integrity, and so it is revealed to Satan by God that Job exceeded the protective hedge with the word "behold." In effect, God says that Job is outside His protective boundary, resulting in tragedy for Job: the loss of his children, wealth, and physical soundness. The main portion of the text consists of the discourse of Job and his three friends concerning why Job was so punished, ending in God answering Job. The Lord blessed the latter days of Job more than his beginning and he lived 140 years according to (Wikipedia) the free encyclopedia. (Job 42:10, 17).

Furthermore, in Chapter 42 of Job:

1. Then Job answered the Lord, and said;
2. I know that thou canst do every thing, and that no purpose can be withholden from thee;
3. Who is he that hideth counsel without knowledge?;
4. Therefore have I uttered that which I understood not, things too wonderful for me, which I knew not. Here I beseech thee, and I will speak: I will demand of thee, and declare thou unto me;
5. I have heard of thee by the hearing of the ear; but now mine eye seeth thee;

6. Wherefore I abhor my words, and repent, seeing I am dust and ashes.
7. And it was so, that after the Lord had spoken these words unto Job, the Lord said to Eliphaz the Temanite: 'My wrath is kindled against thee, and against thy two friends; for ye have not spoken of Me the thing is right, as My servant Job hath. (8) Now therefore, take unto you seven bullocks and seven rams, and go to My servant Job, and offer up for yourselves a burnt offering; and My servant Job shall pray for you; for him will I accept, that I do not unto you aught unseemly; for ye have not spoken of Me the thing that is right, as my servant Job hath. (9) So Eliphaz the Temanite and Bildad the Shuhite and Zophar the Naamathite went, and did according as the Lord commanded them; and the Lord accepted Job. (10) And the Lord changed the fortune of Job, when he prayed for his friends; and the Lord gave twice as much as he had before. (11) Then came there him all his brethren, and all his sisters, and all they had been of his acquaintance before, and did eat bread with him in his house; and the bemoaned him, and comforted him concerning all the evil that the Lord had brought blessed the later end of Job more than his beginning; and he had fourteen thousand sheep, and six thousand camels, and a thousand yoke and oxen, and a thousand she-asses. (13) He had also seven sons and three daughters. (14) And he called the name first, Jeremiah; and the name of the second, Keziah; and the name of the third, Keren-happuch. (15) And all the land were no women found so fair as the daughters of Job; and their father gave him inheritance among their brethren. (16) And after this Job lived a hundred and forty years, and saw his sons, and sons' sons, even four generations. (17) So Job died, being old and full of days.

The Holy Bible: King James Version. 2000
St. Matthew
5
The beginning of the sermon on the mount

1. And seeing the multitudes, he went up into a mountain; and when he was set, his disciples came unto him:
2. And he opened his mouth, and taught them, saying,

The Beatitudes
Lk. 6.20-23

3. Blessed are the poor in spirit: for theirs is the Kingdom of heaven.
4. Blessed are they that mourn: for they shall be comforted. Is 61:2
5. Blessed are the meek: for they shall inherit the earth. Ps. 37.11
6. Blessed are they which do hunger and thirst righteousness: for they shall be filled. Is. 55.1.2
7. Blessed the merciful: for they shall obtain mercy.
8. Blessed are the pure in heart: for they shall see God. Ps 24.4.5
9. Blessed are the peacemakers: for they shall be called the children of God.
10. Blessed are they which are prosecuted for righteousness' sake: 1Pet.3:14
11. Blessed are ye, when men shall revile you, and shall say all manner of evil against you falsely, for my sake. 1Pet.4.14
12. Rejoice, and be exceeding glad: for great is your reward in heaven: for so persecuted they the prophets 2Chr.3616; Act 7.52

The Salt of the Earth

13. Ye are the salt of the earth: but if the salt have lost his savior, wherewith shall it be salted? It is thenceforth good for nothing, but to be cast out, and to be trodden under foot of men. MK 9.50- LK 14.34.35

The Light of the World

14. Ye are the light of the world. Job 8.12;9.5 A city that is set on a hill cannot be hid.
15. Neither do men light a candle, and put it under a bushel, but on a candlestick; MK 4.21:LK8.16:11.33 and giveth light unto all that are in the house.
16. Let you light so shine before men, that they may see your good works, and glorify your Father which is in heaven. 1Pet.2.12

Jesus' Attitude Toward the Law

17. For verily I say unto you, Till heaven and earth pass, one jot or one title shall in no wise pass form the law, till all be fulfilled. LK.16.17

Jesus' Attitude Toward Anger
Lk. 12.57-59

18. Ye have heard that it was said by them of old time, thou shalt not kill; Ex.20.13. Deut.5.17 and whosoever kill shall be in danger of the judgment:
19. But I say unto you, that whosoever is angry with his brother without a cause shall be in danger of the judgment: and whosoever shall say to his brother, Raca, shall be in danger of the council: but whosoever shall say, thou fool, shall be in danger of hell fire.
20. Therefore if thou bring they gift to the alter, and there rememberest that thy bother hath aught against thee;
21. Leave there thy gift before the alter, and go they way; first be reconciled to they brother, and then come and offer thy gift.
22. Agree with thine adversary quickly, while thou art in the way with him; lest at any time the adversary deliver thee to the judge, and the judge deliver thee to the officer, and thou cast into prison.
23. Verily I say unto thee, Thou shalt by no means come out thence, till thou hast paid the uttermost farthing.

Jesus' Attitude Toward Adultery

24. Ye have heard that it was said by them of old time, thou shalt not commit adultery: Ex 29.14. Deut.5.18
25. But I say unto you, That whosoever looketh on a woman to lust after her hath committed adultery with her already in his heart.
26. And if thy right eye offends thee, pluck it out, and cast it from thee: for it is possible for thee that one of thy members should perish, and not that thy whole body should be cast into hell. Mt. 18.19;MK.9.47
27. And if thy right hand offends thee, cut it off, and cast it from thee: for it is profitable for thee that one of they members should perish, and not that thy whole body should be cast into hell. Mt. 18.8' Mk. 9.43

Chapter

4

Success Through Positive Thinking

There have been five transitions that changed my life and brought success through positive thinking: volunteering for the United States Marine Corps; working for the Federal Government; meetings with Ronald Gidwitz, a moderate Republican thinker in the late 1980s; Presbyterian thought, and open heart surgery for aortic stenosis.

The writings on the following pages are meant to give a sprinkling as to how success through positive thinking can motivate and inspire one's everyday thinking and living. It is the hope that this compilation will bring happiness and motivation to you who read them and process the messages. Hopefully, your life will change for the better and bring success through positive thinking.

Affirmations

"In times of despair one must possess passion, responsibility, and empathy to forgo obstacles confronted with in life."

"You are whom you consort with."

—Mel Mahone, Ph.D.

Success through positive thinking starts during an economic downturn, which leads to an economic depression, unemployment, recession, loss of hope, and despair. During these times, one should be:
- Prayerful
- Persistent
- Willing to learn new skills
- Educated
- Cogitative about being an entrepreneur
- Employed, even in a series of part-time jobs
- Zealous
- Motivated
- Meditative
- Prepared to lead rather than follow

Prayerful

Call on, implore, appeal to, entreat, beg petition, (verb) supplicate, devotion, intercession, make one's devotions, offer a prayer. She prayed to God to forgive her.

1. "Hail Mary, full of grace, the Lord is with thee: Blessed art thou among women, and blessed is the fruit of thy womb, Jesus." —Anonymous - Ave Maria, 11th century

2. "O Lord! Thou knowest how busy I must be this day: if I forget thee, do not forget thee, do not thou forget me."—Lord Astley (1579–1652), English Royalist general.

3. "Give me chastity and continence, but not yet." —St. Augustine of Hippo (354–430), Bishop of Hippo

Persistent

(Adjective): tenacious, reserving, determined, resolute, purposeful, dogged, single-minded, tireless, indefatigable, patient, unflagging, untiring, insistent, importunate, relentless, unrelenting, stubborn, intransigent, obstinate, obdurate, formal pertinacious, determination, endurance, and patience. He is a very persistent man.

1. "If the mountain will not come to Mahomet, Mahomet must go to the mountain." —Proverb
2. "Never say die." —Proverb
3. "Slow but sure wins the race."— Proverb
4. "And ye shall be hated of all men for my name's sake: but he that endureth to the end shall be saved." —Bible: Matthew 10:22
5. "If at first you don't succeed, try, try again."—William Edward Hickson (1803–1870), British educator
6. "I am a kind of burr; I shall stick."—William Shakespeare (1564–1616), English dramatist

Learn New Skills

Skill (noun): expertise, skillfulness, expertness, adeptness, adroitness, deftness, dexterity, ability, prowess, mastery, competence, capability, aptitude, artistry, virtuosity, talent.
Bringing up a family gives you many skills, strengths, and gifts.

1. "It takes people a long time to learn the difference between talent and genius, especially ambitious young men and women." —Louisa May Alcott (1832-1888), American novelist
2. "Mediocrity knows nothing higher than itself, but talent instantly recognizes genius." —Sir Arthur Conan Doyle (1856–1930), British writer
3. "Genius does what it must, and talent does what it can." —Edward Bulwer Lytton (1803–1873), British statesman and poet

Educated

Adjective: informed, literate, schooled, tutored, well-read, learned, knowledgeable, enlightened, intellectual, academic, erudite, scholarly, cultivated, cultured, lettered. Her assistant was an educated and creative young man.

1. "Soon learned, soon forgotten." —Traditional Proverb
2. "They know enough who know how to learn." —Henry Brooks Adams (1838–1918), American historian
3. "But above all things I strive to train them to be useful to the Holy Church of God and for the glory of your kingdom." —Alcuin of York (C.735–804), English theologian
4. "Studies serve for delight, for ornament, and for ability." —Sir Frances Bacon (1516–1626), English lawyer and philosopher
5. "The education of the doctor which goes on after he has his degree is, after all, the most important part of his education." —John Shaw Billings (1838–1913), American librarian and surgeon
6. "Education is simply the soul of a society as it passes from one generation to another." —Gilbert K. Chesterton (1874–1976), English journalist and novelist
7. "The most essential part of a student's instruction is obtained, as I believe, not in the lecture room, but at the beside." —Oliver Wendell Holmes (1841–1935), American physician
8. "You sought the last resort of feeble minds with classical educations. You became a school master." —Aldous Huxley (1894–1964), British Novelist and essayist

Cogitative About Being an Entrepreneur

Noun: businessman/businesswoman, enterpriser, speculator, tycoon, magnate, mogul, dealer, trader, promoter, impresario, informal wheeler-dealer, whiz kid, mover and shaker, go-getter, high flyer, hustler, idea man/person. e HweHHe He was young entrepreneur who started a dry cleaning business at the age of 23.

1. "Pile it high, sell it cheap." —Sir John Edward Cohen (1898–1979), British businessman

2. "The business of America is business." —Calvin Coolidge (1872–1933), 30th US president

3. "A business that makes nothing but money is a poor kind of business." —Henry Ford (1863–1947), American businessman and car manufacturer

4. "No nation was ever ruined by trade." —Benjamin Franklin (1706–1790), American statesman

5. "Remember that time is money." —Benjamin Franklin

6. "There's no such thing as a free lunch." —Milton Friedman (1912–2006), American economist

7. "If you pay peanuts, you get monkeys." —James Goldsmith (1933–1997), French businessman

8. "Where wealth and freedom reign, contentment fails, and honor sinks where commerce long prevails." — Oliver Goldsmith (1730–1774), Irish-born British essayist and novelist

9. "He's a businessman...I'll make him an offer he can't refuse." —Mario Puzo (1920–), American novelist

10. "A dinner lubricates business." —William Stowell (1745–1836), British jurist

11. "Right or wrong, the customer is always right."
—Harry Gordon Selfridge (1857–1947) US-born businessman. Also attributed to Marshall Field (1834–1906), American department store owner

Employed (Even in a Series of Part-time Jobs)

Noun, Job: occupation, profession, trade, position, career, work, line of work, livelihood, post, situation, appointment, métier, craft, vocation, calling, vacancy, opening, (humorous: McJob), task, piece of work, assignment, project, chore, undertaking, venture, operation, enterprise, business, responsibility, duty, charge, task, rule, function, mission. My job involves a lot of traveling.

1. "A priest sees people at their best, a lawyer at their worst, but a doctor sees them as they really are." — Traditional Proverb

2. "Every man to his trade." —Proverb

3. "Jack-of-all trades, master on none." —Figure of speech

4. "Old soldiers never die; they just fade away." — Douglas MacArthur (1880–1964), American general

5. "Once a parson always a parson." —Traditional Proverb

6. "Sailors have a port in every storm." —Traditional Proverb

8. "A doctor who doesn't say too many foolish things is patient half-cured, just as a critic is a poet who has stopped writing verse and a policeman a burglar who has retired from practice." —Marcel Proust (1871-1922), French novelist

9. "The best careers advice to give to the young is 'Find out what you like doing best and get someone to pay you for doing it!'" —Katherine Whitehorn (1926–) British journalist

Zealous (adjective): fervent, ardent, fervid, fanatical, passionate, impassioned, devout, devoted, committed, deducted, hard-cure, enthusiastic, eager, keen, overkeen, avid, card-carrying, vigorous, energetic, intense, fierce, literary perfervid. She is a zealous worker.

1. "The person who is master of their passions is reason's slave." —Cyril Connolly (1903–1974), British author

2. "A man who has not passed through the inferno of his passions has never overcome them." —Carl Gustav Jung (1875–1961), Swiss psychiatrist

3. "It is with our passions, as it is with fire and water, they are good servants but bad masters." —Aesop (620 B.C.–560 B.C.), Greek slave and fable author

4. "Give me that man that is not passion's slave, and I will wear him in my heart's core, ay, in my heart of heart, As I do thee." —William Shakespeare (1564-1616), English dramatist and playwright

Motivated (verb): prompt, drive, move, inspire, stimulate, influence. Activate. Impel, push, propel, spur (on), (inspire), stimulate, encourage, spur (on), excite, inspirit, incentivize, fire with enthusiasm. It's the teachers job to motivate the child.

1. "A spur in the head is worth two in the heel.
— Proverb

2. "Ninety percent of inspiration is perspiration."
— Proverb

3. "Inspiration is the act of drawing up a chair to the writing desk." —Anonymous

4. "The true God, the mighty God, is the God of ideas." —Alfred Victor Vigny (1797 –1863), French writer

Meditate (verb): contemplate, think, consider, ponder, muse, reflect, deliberate, ruminate, chew the cud, brood, mull something over, be in a brown study, be deep/lost in thought, debate with oneself, pray, (informal) put on one's thinking cap, (formal) cogitate. Please allow me more time to meditate.

1. "Prayer makes the Christian's armour bright, and Satan trembles when he sees the weakest saint upon his knees." —William Cowper (1731–1800), British poet

2. "Some day when you have time, look into the business of prayer, amulets, baths and poultices, and discover for yourself how much valuable therapy the profession has cast on the dump." —Martin H. Fischer (1879–1962), German-American physician and writer

3. "For when two or three are gathered together in my name there I am among them." —Bible, Matthew 18:20

Lead Rather than Follow

Lead (verb): guide, conduct, show the way, lead the way, usher, escort, steer, pilot, shepherd, accompany, see, take, head the way, take the initiative, break (new) ground, blaze a trail, prepare the way, be at the forefront. He'd lead the way in developing new technologies.

1. "I know that the right kind of political leader for the Labour Party is a desiccated calculating machine."

— Aneurin Bevan (1897–1960), Welsh Labor politician

2. "The trouble in modern democracy is that men do not approach to leadership until they have lost the desire to lead anyone." —Lord William Beveridge (1879–1963), British economist

3. "And he shall rule them with a rod of iron; as the vessels of a potter shall they be broken to shivers: even as I received of my Father." —Bible: Revelations 2:27

4. "Let me pass, I have to follow them, I am their leader." —Alexander Auguste Ledru-Rollin (1807–1874), French lawyer and politician

The Ultimate Resource

Dennis Kimbro and Napoleon Hill, authors of *Think and Grow Rich: A Black Choice*, showed that when asked to describe man's greatest resource, James Allen, the English essayist, told the following tale:

> One day, two successful businessmen were standing on the bridge overlooking Niagara Falls, impressed by the breathtaking view. One turned to the other and said, "Behold the greatest source of undeveloped power in America."
>
> "No!" replied his friend. "America's greatest source of undeveloped power is the soul of man."

In our country, thousands of people of all races try desperately to excuse themselves for their lack achievement. Millions turn their attention toward poverty and failure. Try to uncover any reason for this inactivity and you will hear the following arguments: "It's society's fault," or "The circumstances are beyond my control," or better yet, "You either have it or you don't." Some people view themselves as victims of an unforgiving system rigged for their eventual demise. When you study the unheralded accomplishments of the thousands who have walked out of the ghettos into greatness, you uncover the truth: The poor, despondent victims are actually volunteers who are ignorantly cooperating in their own failure.

Many men and women idle away their lives, waiting for something to turn up or for someone to give them a boost. The greatest evil lies within the minds of those who believe that the world owes them something, or that somebody must help them before they ever start. Let me hasten to remind you of valuable words spoken by the late Napoleon Hill, who emphatically stated, "Start where you stand and work with whatever tools you may have at your command...."

The greatest resources of the world today are not those that lie beneath the earth. Natural resources such as oil, platinum, and yes, even gold, when compared to the resources that each of us has at our disposal, are virtually worthless. The greatest resources are human resources—that is, the need of the human soul to desire, to produce, to be self-reliant.

Langston Hughes, the acclaimed and prolific writer, knew the true meaning of the ultimate resource. Few American writers have had such rich and varied experiences, and few were so indiscriminate in selecting materials for their works. A broken family and a segregated society appeared to offer him little. When life seemed to close its doors, he turned to writing and discovered a different world. Never one to forget his cultural past, Hughes wrote with passion concerning the plight of Black America in the 1930s. So talented was he that the literary world referred to his as "Shakespeare in Harlem."

Though Hughes was the victim of discrimination, his deepest allegiance and hope for the future was distinctively tied to the country of his birth. He wrote in "My America":

> All over America, however, against the Negro there has been an economic color line of such severity that since the Civil War we have been kept most effectively, as a racial group, in the lowest economic brackets...Simply look around you on the Main Street of any American town or city. There are no colored clerks in any of the stores—although colored people spend their money there. There are practically never any colored street-car conductors or bus drivers...There are no colored girls at the switchboards of the telephone company—but millions of Negroes have phones and pay their bills. Even in Harlem, nine times out of ten, the man who comes to collect your rent is white.... Yet America is a land where, in spite of its defects, I can write this article. Here the voice of democracy is still heard....

The Master Key to Riches

What does the process of achievement and progress need more than anything else? It needs self-discipline. What is self-discipline? In the philosophy of success taught by Napoleon Hill, self-discipline might be described as the counter balance of enthusiasm. Self-discipline is the principle that channels your enthusiasm in the right direction.

In the simplest terms, self-discipline is taking control of your mind, your habits, and your emotions. Until you master self-discipline, you cannot be a leader of others and success will evade your grasp. Self-discipline is the ability to do what you should do, when you should do it, whether you want to or not.

Self-Discipline in Action

Characteristics such as a pleasing personality, faith, imagination, persistence, freedom from fear and failure, right mental attitude, and desire are attainable only through self-discipline. Self-discipline is the key quality by which you may voluntarily shape the patterns of thought to be in harmony with your aims and chief purpose. In the field of salesmanship, for example, all master salesmen know that the successful salesman is the persistent salesman. And persistence is a matter of strict self-discipline.

Debi Thomas started skating in secondhand skates so tight her feet ached. To finance her training and constant travel, her mother was forced to skip mortgage payments. In order to reach her goal of competing in the Olympics, Thomas made her own costumes, choreographed her own routines, repaired broken skates with Elmer's glue, and for 12 successive years adhered to the same six-hour-a-day practice routine. Thomas was the first black female to make the US Olympic figure-skating team. She was the first American female skating champion in 30 years to attend college while competing. Raised by her mother, Thomas has always relied on relentless willpower and strict discipline. *In Think and Grow Rich*, she describes her secret of inner strength:

> I've learned at being good at anything-sports, school, or whatever-means devoting time, energy, and effort. It also means making some difficult choices and sacrifices. For me, becoming a world-class figure skater meant long hours of practice while sometimes tolerating painful injuries. It meant being totally exhausted sometimes, and not being able to do all the things I wanted to do when I wanted to do them. But my dream came true. It took some talent, a fair share of luck a good measure of

persistence, but most of all it took a great deal of self-discipline.

Where Does Self-Discipline Lead?

Self-discipline leads to self-actualization. Abraham Maslow, American professor of psychology, defined the self-actualized person as a "person who makes full use of and exploits his talents, potentialities, and capacities. Such a person seems to be fulfilling himself and doing the best he is capable of doing." Maslow further explained that "the self-actualized person must find in his life those qualities that make his living rich and rewarding. He must find meaningfulness, self-sufficiency, effortlessness, playfulness, richness, simplicity, completion, necessity, perfection, individuality, beauty, and truth." This is the whole person—the rich, fulfilled inner person combined with the well-organized complete outer person.

A Call for New Leaders

Anyone who is honest with himself realizes that he has been happiest and most satisfied after having successfully completed a difficult task. A leader is the person who can help others overcome any challenge. A leader is the person who shows by example that any job is worth doing well. A leader is the student who studies to learn, and not just receive a grade. A leader is the neighbor who sets a positive example in his or her community. A leader is the employee who has the sense to realize that he gets the most out of any job by giving loyalty and dedication to the firm that pays his wages. A leader is the person who realizes the importance of becoming a bigger and better person with each passing day. A leader takes the responsibility for his own growth through self-discipline. How can you become a leader? Easy. Fix your eye upon your goal. Visualize it with every ounce of your being, and courageously set out toward it. Know and have faith that what should come to you will come to you. Everything in the universe works on the side of the person who works within nature's laws.

How to Get the Job You Want

While millions of jobless workers were asking for work, one man found a way to be of help. Ask yourself, what has he done? First, he decided exactly on the job and industry he wanted. Second, he specialized; he had selected a particular line of work and decided that was where the future would be. Third, he researched and studied his field of interest. Fourth, he knew his strengths and weaknesses, and emphasized his strengths. And fifth, he set out to prove himself. This he did most diligently.

This process may involve your time and efforts, but the difference in income and advancement can eliminate years of hard work at shamefully low wages. Personal initiative is a trait much admired and if carried out with discretion understanding of what must be achieved puts you in harmony with your peers. If you have a goal in kind, then opportunities for personal initiative are easy to find.

The jack-of-all-trades and master of none was the man who suffered during the Depression. People who knew what they were doing and where they were going through those Depression years like a vessel sails through a storm. It wasn't as comfortable as it could have been, but at least the crossing was a success. And thousands of businesses actually prospered and grew larger during those lean years.

There Is No End to Learning

John Morton-Finney was a remarkable man. He lived to be 109 years old and was the son of a former slave. He served in World War I, became fluent in six foreign languages, earned 11 degrees, taught school until he was 81, and practiced law. He had an unquenchable thirst for knowledge that never abated. In his sixties, he enrolled in college all over again, and earned his fourth bachelor's degree at 75. He attended law school seminars with the wide-eyed eagerness of a freshman.

A very humble man who insisted there was nothing extraordinary about his accomplishments, Morton-Finney read three of four books at a time, making copious notes. In the book-lined study in his house, he was at peace when he read Homer, Cervantes, Pericles, Du Bois, Shakespeare, and Chaucer. Why did he read so desperately? "I can get interested in so many things," he once said. "There is so much to know in this world. And it is such a pleasure for me to learn. Besides, a cultivated man would never say 'I finished my education' because he graduated from college. There is no end to learning."

In his childhood, Morton-Finney learned about his ancestors, who migrated from Ethiopia to Nigeria. Enslaved and brought to America, the family was brought, sold, and separated, only to be enjoyed after the Emancipation Proclamation. Morton-Finney was born in 1889, in Uniontown, Kentucky. The first book he'd ever purchased was Webster's Dictionary. It cost 35 cents—every cent he had—but proved to be a wise investment.

When his mother died, he was sent to Missouri to live with his grandfather and continue his education. The nearest school for blacks was six miles away. Each day, he walked that endless road past a school for whites that was only half as far.

In 1914, he joined the Army and served in Europe. After the war, he immediately enrolled in college and earned bachelor's degrees in mathematics, French, and history. Several years later, when Indiana began to segregate its public schools, Finney taught Greek, Latin, German, Spanish, and French at all-black Crispus Attucks High School, where there were ore teachers with advanced degrees than any other school in the state. Here, he passed on his love for learning and a demanding level for scholarship, while coming to further his education. Every semester, and each summer, he would take a course.

"I had set this ideal," he said. "No child could ask me a question that I couldn't answer or did not know to find the answer." Soon, Morton-Finney had earned master's degrees in education and French from Indiana University. In 1935, he finished his first law degree, to which he would add four more!

When asked to reveal the secrets of his lifelong pursuit of education, Morton-Finney told the story of a bookseller who came to him seeking an order. He was white. The salesman apparently did not think to highly of Morton-Finney teaching black children Latin and Greek.

" I don't believe in a black man getting a white man's education," the salesman said rather curtly.

"And what is a white man's education?" Morton-Finney retorted. After trying to respond to his answerless question, the salesman shrugged his shoulders and left.

"Education is education!" he snapped. Take John Morton-Finney's teaching to heart. Read widely in your chosen field. The public libraries are free. They offer a wide array of organized knowledge on any subject. Attend lectures by respected authorities. Take courses, if available. As the story illustrated, education is a lifelong process and should only end when you do. Think deeply about what you've learned. Digest information for your subconscious to act on. But most importantly, read! Stand out from the crowd. Readers are leaders.

The Thought Factor in Achievement

Philosophical writer James Allen is best known for his book *As a Man Thinketh*, which was first published in 1902. This classic self-help book on positive thinking and personal development shows all that a man achieves and all that he fails to achieve is the direct result of his own thoughts. In a justly ordered universe, where loss of equipoise would mean total destruction, individual responsibility must be absolute. A man's weakness and strength, purity and impurity are his own, and not another man's: they are brought about by himself, and not by another, and they can only be altered by himself, never by another. His condition is also his own, and not another man's. His suffering and his happiness are evolved from within. As he thinks, so he is, as he continues to think, so he remains.

> The universe does not favor the greedy, the dishonest, the vicious, although on the mere surface it may sometimes appear to do so; it helps the honest, the magnanimous, the virtuous. All the great teachers of all the ages have declared this in varying forms, and to prove and know it a man has but to persist in making himself more and more virtuous by lifting up his thoughts.
>
> Intellectual achievements are the result of thought consecrated to the search for knowledge, or for the beautiful and true in life and nature. Such achievements may be sometimes connected with vanity and ambition but they are not the outcome of those characteristics; they are the natural outgrowth of long and arduous effort, and of pure and unselfish thoughts.
>
> Spiritual achievements are the consummation of holy aspirations. He who lives constantly in the conception of noble and lofty thoughts, who dwells upon all that is pure and unselfish, will, as surely as the sun reaches its zenith and the moon its full, become wise and noble in character, and rise into a position of influence and blessedness.
>
> Achievement, of whatever kind, is the crown of effort, the diadem of thought. By the aid of self-control, resolution, purity, righteousness, and well-directed thought a man ascends; by the aid

of animality, indolence, impurity, corruption, and confusion of thought a man descends.

A man may rise to high success in the world, and even to lofty altitudes in the spiritual realm, and again descend into weakness and wretchedness by allowing arrogant, selfish, and corrupt thoughts to take possession of him.

Victories attained by right thought can only be maintained by watchfulness. Many give way when success is assured, and rapidly fall back into failure. All achievements, whether in the business, intellectual or spiritual world, are the result of definitely directed thought, are governed by the same law and are of the same method, the only difference lies in the object of attainment. He who would accomplish little must sacrifice little; he who would achieve much must sacrifice much; he who would attain highly must sacrifice greatly.

Visions and Ideals

Also from *As a Man Thinketh* are valuable observations about visions and ideals.

The dreamers are the saviors of the world. As the visible world is sustained by the invisible, so men, through all their trials and sins and sordid vocations, are nourished by the beautiful visions of their solitary dreamers. Humanity cannot forget its dreamers; it cannot let their ideals fade and die; it lives in them; it knows them in the realities which is shall one day see and know.

Composer, sculptor, painter, poet, prophet, sage, these are the makers of the afterworld, the architects of heaven. The world is beautiful because they have lived, without them, laboring humanity would perish.

He who cherishes a beautiful vision, a lofty ideal in his heart, will one day realize it. Columbus cherished a vision of another world, and he discovered it; Copernicus fostered the vision of a multiplicity of worlds and a wider universe, and he revealed it; Buddha beheld the vision of a spiritual world of stainless beauty and perfect peace, and he entered into it.

Cherish your visions; cherish your ideals; cherish the music that stirs in your heart, the beauty that forms in your mind, the loveliness that drapes your purest thoughts, for out of them will grow all delightful condition, all heavenly environment, of these, if you but remain true to them, your world will at last be built.

To desire is to obtain, to aspire is to achieve. Shall man's basest desires receive the fullest measure of gratification, and his purest aspirations starve for lack of sustenance? Such is not the Law: such a condition of things can never obtain: "ask and receive."

Dream lofty dreams, and as you dream, so shall you become.

Your vision is the promise of what you shall one day be, your ideal is the prophecy of what you shall at last unveil.

The greatest achievement was at first and for a time a dream. The oak sleeps in the acorn; the bird waits in the egg; and in the highest vision of the soul a waking angel stirs. Dreams are the seedlings of realities.

Your circumstances may be uncongenial, but perceive an ideal and strive to reach it. You cannot travel within and stand still without. Here is a youth hard pressed by poverty and labor; confined long hours in an unhealthy workshop; unschooled, and lacking all the arts of refinement. But he dreams of better things; he thinks of intelligence, of refinement of grace and beauty. He conceives of, mentally builds up, an ideal condition of life; the vision of the wider liberty and a larger scope takes possession of him; unrest urges him to action, and he utilizes all his spare time and means, small though they are, to the development of his latent powers and resources. Very soon so altered has his mind become that the workshop can no longer hold him. It has become so out of harmony with his mentality that it falls out of his life as a garment is cast aside, and with the growth of opportunities which fit the scope of his expanding powers, he passes out of it forever. Years later we see this youth as a full-grown man. We find him a master of certain forces of the mind which he wields with world-wide influence and almost unequaled power. In his hands he holds the cords of gigantic responsibilities; he speaks and lo, lives are changed; men and women hang upon his words and remold their characters, and, sun-like, he becomes the fixed and luminous centre round which innumerable destinies revolve. He has realized the Vision of his youth. He has become one with his ideal.

And you, too, youthful reader, will realize the vision (not the idle wish) of your heart, be it base or beautiful, or a mixture of both, for you will always gravitate toward that which you, secretly, must love. Into your hands will be placed the exact results of your own thought; you will receive that which you earn; no more, no less. Whatever your present environment may be, you will fall remain, or rise with your thoughts, your vision, your ideal. You will become as small as your controlling desire; as great as your dominant aspiration; in the beautiful words of Stanton Kirkham Davis, "You may be keeping accounts, and presently you shall walk out of the door that for so long has seemed to you the barrier of your ideals, and shall find yourself before an audience - the pen still behind your ear, the ink stains on your fingers- and then and there shall pour out the torrent of your inspiration. You may be driving sheep and you shall wander to the city- bucolic and open-mouthed; shall wander under the intrepid guidance of the spirit into the studio of the master, and after a time he shall say, 'I have nothing more to teach you.' And now you have become the master, who did so recently dream of great while driving sheep. You shall lay down the saw and the plane to take upon yourself the regeneration of world."

The thoughtless, the ignorant, and the indolent, seeing only the apparent effects of things and not the things themselves, talk of luck, of fortune, and chance. See a man grow rich, they say "How lucky he is!" Observing another become intellectual, they exclaim, "How highly favored he is!" And noting the saintly character and wide influence of another, the remark, "How chance aid him at every turn!" They do not see the trials and failures and struggles which these men have voluntarily encountered in order to gain their experience; have no knowledge of the sacrifices they have made, of the undaunted efforts they have put forth, of the faith they have exercised, that they might overcome the apparently insurmountable, and realize the vision of their heart. They do not know the darkness and the headaches; they only see the light and joy, and call it "luck," do not see the long and arduous journey, but only behold the pleasant goal, and call it "good fortune" do not understand the process, but only perceive the result, and call it chance.

In all human affairs there are efforts, and there are results, and the strength of the effort is the measure of the result. Chance is not. Gifts, powers, material, intellectual, and spiritual possessions are the fruits of effort; they are thoughts completed, objects accomplished, visions realized.

The vision that you glorify in your mind, the ideal that you enthrone in your heart-this you will build your life by, this you will become.

Affirmations for Prosperity

Florence Shovel Shinn, an artist who became a spiritual teacher and a popular writer wrote numerous self-help and motivational books, suggests man comes into the world financed by God, with all that he desires or requires already on his pathway. This supply is released through faith and the spoken word. "If thou canst believe, all things are possible."

In her classic title *The Game of Life and How to Play It*, Shinn gives an example of a woman who came to her one day to tell me of her experience in using an affirmation she had read in her book. "She was without experience but desired a good position on the stage," Shinn writes. "She took the affirmation: 'Indefinite spirit, open the way for my great abundance. I am an irresistible magnet for all that belongs to me by Divine right.' She was given a very important part in a successful opera.

She said: "It was a miracle, due to that affirmation which I repeated hundreds of times."

Affirmations

I now draw from the abundance of the spheres my immediate and endless supply.
All channels are free!
All doors are open!

♦

I now release the gold-mine within me. I am linked with an endless golden stream of prosperity which come to me under grace in perfect ways.

♦

Goodness and mercy shall follow me all the days of my life and I shall dwell in the house of abundance forever.

♦

My God is a God of plenty and I now receive all that I desire or require, and more.

♦

All that is mine by Divine Right is now released and reaches me in great avalanches of abundance, under grace in miraculous ways.

♦

My supply is endless, inexhaustible and immediate and comes to me under grace in perfect ways.

♦

All channels are free and all doors fly open for my immediate and endless, Divinely Designed supply.

♦

My ships come in over a calm sea, under grace in perfect ways.

♦

I give thanks that the millions which are mine by Divine Right, now pour in and pile up under grace in perfect ways.

♦

Unexpected door flys open, unexpected channels are free, and endless avalanches of abundance are poured out upon me, under grace in perfect ways.

♦

I spend money under direct inspiration wisely and fearlessly, knowing my supply is endless and immediate.

♦

I am fearless in letting money go out, knowing God is my immediate and endless supply.

About the Authors

Napoleon Hill was born in 1883 in Virginia and died in 1970 after a long and successful career as a consultant to business leaders, and as a lecturer and an author. His classic *Think and Grow Rich* is the all-time bestseller in its field, having sold tens of million of copies worldwide and setting the standard for today's motivational thinking. His piece "How Success Grows From Failure" first appeared in April 1921 in *Napoleon Hills Magazine*.

James Allen was born in England in 1864. He took his first job at age 15 to support his family, after his father was murdered while looking for work in America. Allen worked as a private secretary with various manufacturing companies until 1902, when he left to devote himself fully to writing. He is widely known for his classic *As a Man Thinketh*. He wrote many well-received books before his death in 1922, the year *Light on Life's Difficulties* was published.

Florence Scovel Shinn (1871–1940) was born in New Jersey and spent many years working as an artist and illustrator of children's literature in New Your City before publishing her new-thought classic *The Game of Life and How to Play It* in 1925. Her affirmations for prosperity appeared in her 1928 sequel, *Your Word Is Your Wand*.

Chapter

5

Motivation and Get Motivated

New York Times bestselling author Tamara Lowe, *Get Motivated!*, points out that you can motivate yourself and others, quickly and easily. As an educator and businesswoman, she conducted an 8-year study on more than 10,000 people. It is a research-based, systematic approach to achievement— and it works.

People are highly motivated by others that they follow in their environment.

Most of us have been as successful as we would like - and I believe there is a reason for that. We simply didn't know how to harness the power of motivation. After all, motivation is difficult to understand. One day we feel motivated...and then the next day we don't. We can be fired up in the morning but burned out by lunchtime. When we feel motivated, we're not sure why. Even, worse, we never know how long our motivation will last.

And when we are unmotivated we usually have no idea how to stir up energy and excitement.

Motivation is unpredictable. It seems to come and go, as random and fleeting as the wind.

The mystery of motivation has puzzled educators, employees, and behavioral scientists for centuries. How can managers inspire their employees and their teams to be more productive? What is the best way for parents to motivate their children?

It is my firm belief that if you consort with "highly motivated people, you will become prone to be a motivated person yourself. You are whom you consort with. If one consorts with highly motivated people, he will be prone for greatness and comfort of life by being motivated.

Motivation comes after learning from your environment to accomplish and to be very interested in following motivated people. Motivation is learned behavior by positioning yourself to learn from the ones that are motivated.

In her book, Lowe outlines that Motivational DNA is made of Drives, Needs, and Awards:

D: Drives
Connection
Production

N: Needs
Stability
Variety

A: Awards
Internal
External

All six of these motivators (connection, production, stability, variety, internal awards, and external awards) inspire

everyone. In Lowe's Model of Motivation, the motivators are defined as:
Need
Creates desire to fulfill needs (food, friendship, recognition, and achievement)

Behavior
Results in actions to fulfill needs

Rewards
Satisfy needs, intrinsic or extrinsic rewards

Feedback
Reward informs person whether behavior was appropriate and should be used again.

Motivation

In the article "The Motivated Project," which outlines challenges managers face with regards to motivating their team members, Brad Hierstetter suggests a simple definition of motivation is the ability to change behavior. It is a drive that compels one to act because human behavior is directed toward theory. "To further complicate matters, some motivational theories clearly contradict others, and a manager's ability to motivate is, to no small degree, related to his or her leadership approach and interpersonal skills. One thing is certain, though: workforce and workplace dynamics are such that there is no one-size-fits-all approach to motivating team members."

Following motivated people and being motivated is learned behavior. It does not happen overnight. One has to benefit from the motivated leaders that they follow. "It is very important to recognize that motivation is an intrinsic phenomenon. According to noted industrial psychologist Frederick Herzberg "extrinsic satisfaction only leads to movements, not motivation." Motivated team members, on the other hand, possess an internal drive that causes them to consistently direct high levels of effort toward completing their project assignments."

Motivational Theories

From "the Motivated Project Team":

> Motivational theories are generally categorized as "content" and "process." Content theories examine factors within individual that stimulate, inspire, and stop behavior. Processes, theories, on the other hand, consider how individuals make decisions and how rewards influence future performance. What follows are some key motivators stemming from common content theories and common process theories (derived from *Human Aspects of Project Management: Human Resource Skills for the Project Manager*, vol.2, Vijay Verma).

Content Theories of Motivation

Content theories of motivation examine factors within individuals that stimulate, inspire, and stop behavior.

Achievement Theory
Team members can be motivated by:
- Suitable role models
- Empowerment
- Financial incentives that match level of achievement
- Regular, constructive feedback.

Hierarchy of Needs (Abraham H Maslow)
Team members can be motivated by:
- A comfortable, participative, and safe project environment
- Challenging assignments
- Recognition for exceptional performance

Motivator/Hygiene Theory (Fredrick Herzberg)
Herzberg believe that motivators such as the following can increase job satisfaction:

- Challenging assignment
- Increased responsibility
- The possibility of achievement, advancement, personal growth, or recognition

Herzberg also believed that factors such as compensation, level of supervision, relationships with coworkers and superiors, and working conditions do not always foster motivation; however, not providing them can create job dissatisfaction.

Process Theories of Motivation
Process theories of motivation consider how individuals make decisions and how rewards influence future performance.

Contingency Theory (John J. Morse and Jay W. Horsch)
Team members can be motivated when:

- The tasks they are expected to perform align well to their individual skills
- The degree of freedom granted them by management, as characterized by the formality of their work environment and the degree to which they are empowered matches the type of work being done.

When team members' skill sets are not sufficient for the job at hand, they should be provided training that will enhance their overall competence.

Equity Theory (John S. Adams)
Team members' motivation can be influenced by the perception of how fairly rewards are distributed throughout

the organization. Unfair allocation of rewards, whether actual or perceived, can negatively impact team member motivation.

Expectancy Theory (Victor H. Vroom)
Team members may exhibit greater effort when they feel that this effort will result in a favorable outcome or a desired reward. Implicit, here, is the notion that people give serious thought to how much effort they wish to expend before performing a task.

Goal-Setting Theory (Gary P. Latham and Edwin A. Locke)
Team members can be motivated by goals that are both precise and challenging. A participative approach to goal formulation that includes project team members can foster greater team member commitment toward achieving goals.

Reinforcement Theory (B. F. Skinner's behavior modification theories)
Team members can be motivated when desirable behaviors are encouraged (using positive reinforcement) by providing them with incentives that they value. Examples of incentives include:

- Access to better equipment
- Challenging assignment
- Increased independence
- Job promotions
- Sincere praise

Undesirable behaviors can be discouraged by punishment.

Theory X and Theory Y (Douglas McGregor)
Theory X promulgates the notion that team members will follow the path of least resistance and are largely motivated by money, punishment, or station.

Theory Y, on the other hand, generally assumes that team members are committed to organizational goals, are self-disciplined, desire increased responsibility, and will meet expectations if properly motivated and afforded a supportive work environment.
Most project team members fit Theory Y assumptions.

Theory Z (William G. Ouchi)
Similar to the Theory Y managers described by McGregor, Theory Z managers generally trust their team members. Managers can foster increased levels of motivation and productivity by exhibiting high levels of confidence, commitment, and trust in project team members.

Need Theories

Need theories are based on some of the earliest research in the field of human relations. The premise behind need theories is that if managers can understand the needs that motivate people, then reward systems can be implemented that fulfill those needs and reinforce the appropriate behavior.

Hierarchy of Needs

Abraham Maslow, a professor at Brandeis University and a practicing psychologist, developed the Hierarchy of Needs Theory. He identified a set of needs that he prioritized into a hierarchy based on two conclusions (Daft, 1997; McCoy, 1992; Quick, 1985):
1. Human needs are either of an altercation, desire nature or of an avoidance nature.
2. Because humans are "wanting" being, when one desire is satisfied, another desire will take its place.

Maslow's Hierarchy of Needs
- Self-Actualization
- Esteem

- Belongingness and Love
- Security/Safety
- Physiological

Physiological: These are basic physical comfort or bodily needs: food, sex, drink, and sleep, in the workplace, these needs translate into a safe, ergonomically designed work environment with an appropriate base salary compensation.

Security/Safety: People want to feel safe, secure, and free from fear. They need stability, structure, and order. In the workplace, job security and fringe benefits, along with an environment free of violence, fills these needs.

Belongingness and love: This is a need for friends, family, and intimacy; for social acceptance and affection from one's peers. In the workplace, this need is satisfied by participation in work groups with good relationships among coworkers and between workers and managers.

Esteem: People want the esteem of others and they want to be regarded as useful, competent, and important. People also desire self-esteem and need a good self-image. In the workplace, increased responsibility, high status, and recognition for contributions satisfy these needs.

Self-Actualization: The highest motivation level involves people striving to actualize their full potential, to become more of what they are capable of being. They seek to attain self-fulfillment. In the workplace, people satisfy this need by being creative, receiving training, or accepting challenging assignments.

Chapter 6

Inspiration About Life

In *The Game of Life and How to Play It*, Florence Scovel Shinn indicates: "Most people consider life a battle, it is a game. It is a game, however, which cannot be played successfully without the knowledge of spiritual law, and the Old and the New Testaments give the rules of the game with wonderful clearness. Jesus Christ taught that it was a great game of giving and receiving." Below is more from the chapter titled "The Game."

> "Whatsoever a man soweth that shall he also reap." This means that whatever man sends out in word or deed, will return to him; what it gives, he will receive. If he gives hate, he will receive hate; if he gives love, he will receive love; if he gives criticism, he will receive criticism; if he lies he will be lied to; if he cheats he will be cheated. We are taught also, that the imaging faculty plays a leading part in the game of life.
>
> "Keep thy heart (or imagination) with all diligence, for out of it are the issues of life." (Prov. 4:23)

There are three departments of the mind, the subconscious, conscious and superconscious. The subconscious, is simply power, without direction. It is like steam or electricity, and it does what it is directed to do; it has no power of induction.

Whatever man feels deeply or images clearly, is impressed upon the subconscious mind, and carried out in minutest detail. For example: a woman I know, when a child, always "made believe" she was a widow. She "dressed up" in black clothes and wore a long black veil, and people thought she was very clever and amusing. She grew up and married a man with whom she was deeply in love. In a short time he died and she wore black and a sweeping veil for many years. The picture of herself as a widow was impressed upon the subconscious mind, and in due time worked itself out, regardless of the havoc created.

The conscious mind has been called mortal or carnal mind.

It is the human mind sees life as it appears to be. It sees death, disaster, sickness, poverty and limitation of every kind, and it impresses the subconscious.

The superconscious mind is the God Mind within each man, and is the realm of perfect ideas.

Many people, however, are in ignorance of their true destinies and are striving for things and situations, which do not belong to them, and would only bring failure and dissatisfaction if attained. For example: A woman came to me and asked me to "speak the word" that she would marry a certain man with whom she was very much in love. (She called him A.B.) I replied that this would be a violation of spiritual law, but that I would speak the word for the right man, the "divine selection," the man who belonged to her by divine right.

I added, "If A.B. is the right man you can't lose him, and if he isn't you will receive his equivalent." She saw A.B. frequently had no headway was made in their friendship. On evening she called, and said, "Do you know, for the last week, A.B. hasn't seemed so wonderful to me." I replied, "Maybe he is not the divine selection—another man may be the right one." Soon after that, she met another man who fell in love with her at once, and who said she was his ideal. In fact, he said all the things that she had always wished A.B. would say to her. She soon returned his love, and lost all interest in A.B. This shows the law of substitution. A right idea was substituted for a wrong one, therefore there was no loss or sacrifice involved.

Jesus Christ said, "Seek ye first the Kingdom of God and his righteousness; and all these things shall be added unto you," and he said the Kingdom was within man.

The Kingdom is the realm of right ideas, or the divine pattern.

Jesus Christ taught that man's words played a leading part in the game of life. "By your words ye are justified and by your words ye are condemned...."

The object of the game of life is to see clearly one's good and to obliterate all mental pictures of evil. This must be done by impressing the subconscious mind with a realization of good. A very brilliant man, who has attained great success, told me he had suddenly erased all fear from his consciousness by reading a sign which hung a the room. He saw printed, in large letters this statement— "Why worry, it will probably never happen." These words were stamped indelibly upon his subconscious mind, and he has now a firm conviction that only good can come into his life, therefore only good can manifest.

Napoleon Hill and W. Clement Stone ask, in *Success Through Positive Mental Attitude*, "Can you attract happiness?" Abraham Lincoln once remarked, "It has been my observation that most folks just are about as happy as they make up their minds to be." In the book, the authors state, "There is very little difference in people, but that little difference makes a big difference! The little difference is attitude. The big difference is whether it is positive or negative."

Persons who want to be happy will adopt a positive mental attitude and be influenced by the PMA side of their talisman. Thus happiness will be attracted to them. And those who turn on NMA make a business of being unhappy. They don't attract—they repel happiness.

"I want to be happy...." A popular song starts off with words that contain a great deal of truth: "I want to be happy, but I won't be happy, "til I make you happy, too!"

One of the surest ways to find happiness for yourself is to devote your energies toward making someone else happy. Happiness is an elusive, transitory thing. And if you set out to search for it, you will find it evasive. But if you try to bring happiness to someone else, then it comes to you.

Writer Claire Jones, wife of a professor in the religion department at Oklahoma City University, tells of a happiness they experienced during their married life. "We lived in a small town the first two years we were married," she recalls, "and our neighbors were a very old couple, the wife nearly blind and confined to a wheelchair. The old man, Not very well himself, kept house and cared for her.

"My husband and I were decorating our Christmas tree a few days before Christmas, when we decided on impulse to fix a tree for the old people. We bought a small one, decorated it with tinsel and lights, wrapped a few small gifts, and took it over the night before Christmas.

"The old lady cried as she gazed dimly at the sparkling lights. Her husband said over and over, "But it's been years since we had a tree." They mentioned that tree nearly every time we visited them during the next year.

"The next Christmas they were both gone from the little house. It was a small thing we had done for them. But we were happy that we'd done it."

Now the happiness they experienced as a result of their kindness was a very deep, warm feeling the memory of which will remain with them. It was a very special kind of happiness that comes to those that want kind deeds.

But the kind of happiness which is most common and most constant comes closer to being a state of contentment: a state of being neither happy nor unhappy.

You are happy person during a period when you predominately experience that positive state of mind in which you are happy combined with the natural state of mind in which you are unhappy... For the choice is yours. The determining factor is whether you are under the influence of a positive or negative mental attitude. And that factor you can control.

"Handicaps are no barrier to happiness," Hill and Stone continue. "Surely if ever there was a person who might have been expected to complain of unhappiness Helen Keller was that person. Born deaf, mute, and blind deprived of knowledge of normal communication with the persons who surrounded her, She had only her sense of touch to help her to reach out to others and to experience the happiness of loving and being loved."

But reach out she did, and through the aid of a devoted and brilliant teacher who in love reached out to Helen Keller, that deaf, mute, and blind little girl became a brilliant, joyful, happy woman. Miss Keller once wrote: *

"Anyone who out of the goodness of his heart speaks a helpful word, gives a cheering smile, or smoothes over a rough place in another's path knows that the delight he feels is so intimate a part of himself that he lives by it. The joy of surmounting obstacles which once seemed unremovable, and pushing the frontier of accomplishment further—what joy is there like unto it?

"If those who seek happiness would stop one little minute and think, they would see that the delights they already experience are as countless as the grasses at their feet, or the dew drops sparkling upon the morning flowers."

Helen Keller counts her blessings and is profoundly grateful for them. Then she shares the wonder of these blessings with others, and causes them to feel delight. Because she shares that which is good and desirable, she attracts unto herself more of that which is good and desirable. For the more you share, the more you will have. And if you share happiness with others, happiness will grow richer within you.

But if you share misery and unhappiness, you will attract misery and unhappiness to yourself. And we all know of persons who are eternally having troubles—not problems, or opportunities in disguise. Theirs are spelled t-r-o-u-b-l-e. No matter what happens to them, it just isn't good. And this is because they are always sharing their troubles with others.

Now there are many lonely people in the world who long for love and friendship but never seem to get it. Some repel that which they seek with NMA. Others curl up in their little corners and never venture out. They secretly hope that something good will come to them, but they do not share any of the good which they enjoy. They do not realize that when you withhold from others that which you have which is good and desirable, your own portion of the good and desirable diminishes.

Others, however, have the courage to do something about their loneliness, and they find their answer in sharing the good and beautiful with others. There was one such little boy who was a very lonely, unhappy little boy indeed. When he was born his backbone was arched into a grotesque hump and his left leg was crooked. Looking at the infant, the doctor assured the boy's father: "But he'll get along all right...."

The family was poor. And the baby's mother died before he was a year old. As he grew up, other children shunned him because of his misshapen body and his inability to participate successfully in many of their activities. Charles Steinmetz was his name... Charles worked hard, long and earnestly. During his lifetime he patented more than 200 electrical inventions and wrote many books and papers on problems of electrical theory and engineering. He knew the satisfaction of making contributions which went far to make this world a better place... Thus Steinmetz experienced the happiness of a full and useful life.

*From *The Open Door*, by Helen Keller. Used by permission of Doubleday & Co; Inc.

Hill suggests in *The Law of Success* that the six most dangerous enemies that can effect your well-being are labeled: Fear of Poverty, Fear of Death, Fear of Ill-Health, Fear of the Loss of Love, Fear of Old Age, and Fear of Criticism. The Fear of Poverty requires courage to tell the truth about the history of this enemy of mankind, and still greater courage to hear the truth after it has been told. The Fear of Poverty grows out of man's habit of preying upon his fellow men, economically. The animals, which have instinct, but no power to think, prey upon one another physically. Man, with his superior sense of intuition, and his more powerful weapon of thought, does not eat his fellow man bodily; he gets more pleasure from eating him financially."

So great an offender is man, in his respect, that nearly every sate and nation has been obliged to pass laws, scores of laws, to protect the weak from the strong. Every blue-sky law is indisputable evidence of man's nature to prey upon his weaker brother economically. The second of man's fears is Fear of Death.

The Fear of Death! For tens of thousands of years man has been asking the still unanswered questions—"Whence?" and "Whither?" The more crafty of the race have not been slow to offer the answer to this eternal question, "Where did I come from and where I am going after Death?" "Come into my tent," says one leader, "and you may go to Heaven after Death." Heaven was then pictured as a wonderful city whose streets were lined with gold and studded with precious stones. "Remain out of my tent and you may go straight to hell." Hell was then pictured as a blazing furnace where the poor victim might have the misery of burning forever brimstone. No wonder mankind FEARS DEATH!

The Fear of Ill Health: This fear is born of both physical and social heredity. From birth until death there is eternal warfare within every physical body; warfare between groups of cells, one group being known as the friendly builders of the body, and the other as the destroyers, or "disease germs." The seed of fear is born in the physical body, to begin with, as the result of Nature's cruel plan of permitting the stronger forms of cell life to prey upon the weaker. Social heredity has played its part through lack of cleanliness and knowledge of sanitation. Also, through the law of suggestion cleverly manipulated by those who profited by ILL HEALTH.

The Fear of Loss of Love of Someone: This fear fills the asylums with the insanely jealous, for jealously is nothing but a form of insanity. It also fills the divorce courts and causes murders and other forms of cruel punishment. It is a holdover, handed down through social heredity, from the Stone Age when man preyed upon his fellow man by stealing his mate by physical force. The method, but not the practice, has now changed to some extent. Instead of physical force man now steals his fellow man's mate with pretty colorful ribbons and fast motor cars and bootleg whisky, and sparkling rocks and stately mansions. Man is improving. He now "entices" where once he "drove." The fifth of man's fears is The Fear of Old Age.

The Fear of Old Age! This fear grows out of two major causes. First, the thought that old age may bring with it poverty. Secondly, from false and cruel sectarian teachings which have been so well mixed with fire and brimstone that every human being learned to fear old age because it meant the approach of another and, perhaps, a more horrible world than this.

The Fear of Criticism: Just how and where man got this fear is difficult to determine, but it is certain that he has it. But for this fear men would not become bald-headed. Bald heads come from tightly fitting hat-bands, which cut off the circulation from the roots of the hair. Women seldom are bald because they wear loose fitting hats. But for Fear of Criticism man would lay aside his hat and keep his hair.

The makers of clothing have not been slow to capitalize this basic Fear of Mankind. Every season the style change, because the clothes makers know that few people have the courage to wear a garment that is one season out of step with what "They are all wearing." If you doubt (you gentlemen) start down the street with last year's narrow-brimmed straw hat on, when this year's style calls for the broad brim. Or (you ladies) take a walk down the street on Easter morning with last year's hat on. Observe how uncomfortable you are, thanks to your unseen enemy, the Fear of Criticism.

Hill further suggests that "from the standpoint of society, the world may be divided into leaders and followers. The professions have their leaders; the financial world has its leaders. In all this leadership it is difficult, if not impossible, to separate from the element of pure leadership that selfish element of personal gain or advantage to the individual, without which any leadership would lose its value.

"It is in military service only, where men freely sacrifice their lives for a faith, where men are willing to suffer and die for the right or the prevention of a wrong, that we can hope to realize leadership in its most exalted and disinterested sense....

Leadership, he states, is a composite of a number of qualities "and a major quality is self-confidence."

Self-confidence results, first, from exact knowledge: second, the ability to impart that knowledge; and third, the feeling of superiority over others that naturally follows. All these give the officer poise. To lead, you must *know!* You may bluff all of your men some of the time, but you can't do it all the time. Men will not have confidence in an officer unless he knows his business, and he must know it from the ground up.

The officer should know more about paper work than his first sergeant and company clerk put together; he should know more about messing than his mess sergeant; more about diseases of the horse than his troop farrier. He should be at least as good as any man in his company.

There is no substitute for accurate knowledge.

Hill notes, "Success, as has been stated in dozens of different ways throughout this course, is very largely a matter of tactful and harmonious negotiation with other people. Generally speaking, the man who understands how to 'get people to do things' he wants done may succeed in any calling.

"As a fitting climax for this lesson, on the Law of Concentration, we shall describe the principles through which men are influenced; through which cooperation is gained; through which antagonism is eliminated and friendliness developed."

Force sometimes gets what appear to be satisfactory results, but force, alone, never has built and never can build enduring success.

The world war has done more than anything which has happened in the history of the world to show us the futility of force as a means of influencing the human mind. Without going into details or recounting the instances which could be cited, we all know that force was the foundation upon which German philosophy has been built during the past forty years. The doctrine that might make right was given a worldwide trial and it failed.

The human body can be imprisoned or controlled by physical force, but it is not so with the human mind. No man on earth can control the mind of a normal, healthy person if that person chooses to exercise the God-given right to control his own mind. The majority of people do not exercise this right. They go through the world, thanks to our faulty educational system, without having discovered the strength which lies dormant in their own minds. Now and then something happens, more in the nature of an accident than anything else, which awakens a person and causes him to discover where his real strength lies and how to use it in the development of industry or one of the professions.

In Lesson 13, on "Failure," Hill suggests, "Under ordinary circumstances the term 'failure' is a negative term. In the lesson, the word will be given a new meaning, because the word has been a very much-misused one; and, for that reason, it has brought unnecessary grief and hardship to millions of people.

"In the outset, let us distinguish between 'failure' and 'temporary defeat.' Let us see if that which is so often looked upon as failure is not, in reality, but temporary defeat. Moreover, let us see if this temporary defeat is not usually a blessing in disguise, for that reason that it brings us up with a jerk and redirects our energies along different and more desirable lines."

Neither temporary defeat nor adversity amounts to failure in the mind of a person who looks upon it as a teacher that will teach some needed lesson. As a matter of fact, there is a great and lasting lesson in every reverse, and in every defeat; and, usually, it is a lesson that could be learned in no other way through defeat.

Defeat often talks to us in a "dumb language" that we do not understand. If this were not true, we would not make the same mistakes over and over again without profiting by the lessons that might teach us. If it were not true, we would observe more closely the mistakes, which other people make and profit by them....

Perhaps I can best help you to interpret the meaning of defeat by taking over some of my own experiences covering a period of approximately thirty years. Within this period, I have come to the turning point, which the uninformed call "failure," seven different times. At each of these seven turning points I thought I had made a dismal failure; but now I know that what looked to be a failure was nothing more than a kindly, unseen hand, that halted me in my chosen course and with great wisdom forced me to redirect my efforts along more advantageous pathways.

I arrived at this decision, however, only after I had taken a retrospective view of my experiences and had analyzed them in light of many years of sober and meditative thought.

There's a Sanskrit proverb that I find inspiring that says: "Yesterday is but a dream, tomorrow is only a vision. But today well-lived makes every yesterday a dream of happiness, And every tomorrow a vision of hope. Look well, therefore, to this day."

In his book *Napoleon Hill's Golden Rules*, the author who is considered one of the great writers of personal-success literature, writes, "The term auto-suggestion simply means self-suggestion, suggestion which one deliberately makes to oneself."

James Allen, in his excellent little magazine, *As a Man Thinketh*, has given the world a fine lesson in auto-suggestion by having shown that a man may literally make himself over through this process of self-suggestion.

This lesson, like James Allen's magazine, is intended mainly as a means of stimulating men and women to the discovery and perception of the truth that "they themselves are makers of themselves," by virtue of the thoughts which they choose and encourage; that mind is the master weaver, both of the inner garment of character and the outer garment of circumstance; and that as they have hitherto woven in ignorance, pain, and grief, they may now weave in enlightenment and happiness.

This lesson is not a preachment, nor is it a treatise on morality or ethics. It is a scientific treatise through which the student may understand the reason why the first rung in the magic ladder to success we placed there, and how to make the principle back of that rung a part of his or her own working equipment with which to master life's most important economic problems.

Hill states that this lesson is based upon the following facts:

1. Every movement of the human body is controlled and directed by thought, that is, by orders sent out from the brain, where the mind has its seat of government.

2. The mind is divided into two sections, one being called the conscious section (which directs our bodily activities while we are awake), and the other being called the subconscious section, which controls our bodily activity while we are asleep.
3. The presence of any thought or idea in one's conscious mind (and probably the same is true of thoughts and ideas in the subconscious division of the mind) tends to produce an "associated feeling" and to urge one to appropriate bodily activity in transforming the thought so held into physical reality. For example, one can develop courage and self-confidence by the use of the following, or some similar positive statement, or by holding the thought of this statement in one's mind constantly: "I believe in myself. I am courageous. I can accomplish whatever I undertake. This is called auto-suggestion."

We shall now proceed to give you the modus operandi through which the first step in the magic ladder to success can be appropriated and used. To begin with, search diligently until you find the particular work to which you wish to devote your life, taking care to see that you select that which will profit all who are affected by your activities. After you have decided what your life work is to be, write out a clear statement of it and then commit it to memory.

Several times a day, and especially just before going to sleep at night, repeat the words of a written description of your life work, and affirm to yourself that you are attracting to you the necessary forces, people, and material things with which to attain the object of your life work, or your definite aim in life.

Bear in mind that your brain is literally a magnet, and that it will attract to you other people who harmonize, in thought and in ideals, with those thoughts which dominate your mind and those ideals which are most deeply seated in you.

There is a law, which we may properly call the law of attraction, through the operation of which water seeks its level, and everything throughout the universe of like nature seeks its kind. If it were not for this law, which is immutable as the law of gravitation which keeps the planets in their proper places, the cells out of which an oak tree grows might scamper away and become mixed with the cells out of which the popular grows, thereby producing a tree that would be part popular and part oak. But, such a phenomenon has never been heard of.

Following this law of attraction a little further, we can see how it works out among men and women. We know that successful, prosperous men of affairs seek the companionship of their own kind, while the down-and-outer seeks his kind, and this happens just as naturally as water flows downhill.

Like attracts like, a fact which is indisputable.

Then, if it is true that men are constantly seeking the companionship of those ideals and thoughts harmonize with their own, can you not see the importance of so controlling and directing your thoughts and ideals that you will eventually develop exactly the kind of "magnet" in your brain that you wish to serve as an attraction in drawing others to you?

If it is true that the very presence of any thought in your conscious mind has a tendency to arouse you to bodily, muscular activity that will correspond with the nature of the thought, can you not see the advantage of selecting, with care, the thoughts which you allow your mind to dwell upon?

Read these lines carefully, and think over and digest the meaning which they convey, because we are now laying the foundation for a scientific truth which constitutes the very foundation upon which all worthwhile human accomplishment is based. We are beginning, now, to build the roadway over which you will travel out of the wilderness of doubt, discouragement, uncertainty, and failure, and we want you to familiarize yourself with every inch of this road.

No one knows what thought is, but every philosopher and every man of scientific ability who has given any study to the subject is in accord with the statement that thought is a powerful form of energy which directs the activities of the human body, that every idea held in the mind through prolonged, concentrated thought takes on permanent form and continues to affect the bodily activities according to its nature, either consciously or unconsciously.

Auto-suggestion, which is nothing more or less than an idea held in the mind, through thought, is the only known principle through which one may literally make oneself over, after any pattern he or she may choose.

Under the heading "The Power of Your Mind," Hill further states, "The human mind is a composite of many qualities and tendencies. It consists of likes and dislikes, optimism and pessimism, hatred and love, constructiveness and destructiveness, kindness and cruelty. The mind is made up of all these qualities and more. It is a blending of them all, some minds showing one of these qualities dominating and other minds showing others dominating." More from that section:

Learn How to Use that Wonderful Mind of Yours

The dominating qualities are largely determined by one's environment, training, and associates, and particularly by one's own thoughts! Any thought held constantly in the mind, or any thought dwelt upon through concentration and brought into the conscious mind often, attracts to it those qualities of the human mind it most resembles.

A thought is like a seed planted in the ground in that it brings back a crop after its kind multiplies, and grows; therefore, it is dangerous to allow the mind to hold any thought which is destructive. Such thoughts must sooner or later seek release through physical action.

Through the principle of auto-suggestion—that is, thoughts held in the mind and concentrated upon — any thought will soon begin to crystallize into action.

If the principle of auto-suggestion were generally understood and taught in the public schools, it would change the whole moral and economic standards of the world inside of twenty years. Through this principle, the human mind can rid itself of its destructive tendencies by constantly dwelling upon its constructive tendencies. The qualities of the human mind need the sunlight of nourishment and use to keep them alive. Throughout the universe, there is a law of nourishment and use which applies to everything that lives and grows. This law has decreed that every living thing which is neither nourished nor used must die, and this applies to the qualities of the human mind which we have mentioned.

The only way to develop any quality of the mind is to concentrate upon it, think about it, and use it. Evil tendencies of the mind can be blotted out by starving them to death through disuse!

What would it be worth to the young, plastic mind of the child to understand this principle and commence to make use of it early in life, beginning with kindergarten?

The principle of autosuggestion is one of the fundamental major laws of applied psychology. Through a proper understanding of this principle and with the cooperation of the writers, philosophers, schoolteachers, and preachers, the whole tendency of the human mind can be directed toward constructive effort inside of twenty years or less.

What are you going to do about it?

May it not be a good plan, as far as you are concerned individually, to wait for someone to start a movement for general education along this line, but commence now to make use of this principle for the benefit of you and yours?

Your children may not be fortunate enough to receive this training in school, but there is nothing to hinder you from giving it to them in your home.

You may have been unfortunate in that you never had an opportunity to study and understand the principle of auto-suggestion when you were going to school, but there is nothing to hinder you from studying, understanding, and applying to your own efforts this principle from now on.

Learn something about the wonderful machine which we call the human mind. It is your real source of power. If you are ever to free yourself of petty worries and financial want, it will be through the efforts of that wonderful mind of yours.

There is nothing that savors of occultism in the human mind. It functions in harmony with the physical and economic laws and principles. You do not need the assistance of any person on earth in the manipulation of your mind so it will function as you want it to. Your mind is something which you control, no matter what your station in life may be, provided always that you exercise the right instead of permitting others to do so for you. Learn something of the powers of your mind. It will free you of the curse of fear and fill you with inspiration and courage.

Chapter

7

Being a Bureaucrat and in Government Employment

A Chronological Biography
United States Marine Corps
1969-1970

My life's experiences would suggest that on June 6, 1969, I started being a bureaucrat by serving our country in the United States Marine Corps. While on a 747 plan from Chicago, Illinois, to San Diego, California, I met fellow Navy recruits. The Marine recruits mocked and made fun of the Navy recruits because their drill instructors (DIs) were polite and courteous toward them on the plane. Whereas with the Marine recruits, they hollered, screamed, cursed, and made us feel like we were less than human. It was a cloudy, gloomy, foggy day; on our way the Marine training, we were pushed onto trucks with the driver driving at excess speeds up to 80 mph to our destination. I was 17 years old. I was scared; flying in a plane for first time in my life.

I joined the Marine Corps voluntarily because I was patriotic. I also wanted to leave the gang violence on the streets of the West Side of Chicago. The Marine Corps boot camp was probably the most challenging, arduous, stringent, and difficult training I have ever experienced in my entire life. This training shaped my overall personality for life. I would never be the same scrawny, scared little boy again. Boot camp made shaped my manhood. The Marine Corps made leaders, they trained recruits to follow orders to the letter. It also motivated us. The day in boot camp started by awakening us without fail at 5:00 a.m. every morning; breakfast was served at 6:00 a.m. The Marine Corps DIs screamed regimented orders. I was made to be obedient at the slightest order. I was made to say "Sir," as that seemed the first sound coming from my voice. Never tell the DI "I" or "You"; if I said either of those words I would find myself getting off the ground or deck after being hit by the DI. I was regularly punched and beaten by white recruits and DI's. I was recycled to three different motivation platoons.

 I exercised in 90-degree heat and marched following the cadence of the DI's order. I gained 20 pounds in boot camp. I entered boot camp weighing 130 pounds and graduated weighing 150 pounds. Due to me jerking the trigger with my MK rifle at the rifle range, my sadistic brother, Michael Mahone, one of my rifle instructors, made the DI punch an M16 bullet in my trigger finger. The trigger finger bled, and I didn't jerk the trigger anymore. I qualified on the range pre-qualification day but didn't qualify on qualification day. I was scared and nervous.

 During boot camp training, I was stomped by a white DI because I refused to do push-ups with my M16 between my knuckles on the deck. With every push-up, ones knuckles bled. When my knuckles bled, I stopped doing push-ups. The DI stopped the other recruits from exercising.

 I learned to swim, fire weapons, exercise routines, combat maneuvers, hand-to-hand combat, simulated gunfire, and other boot-camp training essentials. I knew the demanding training was significant and meaningful. Upon graduating from the Marine Corps boot camp, our platoon won an award and made an honor platoon. Gunnery Sgt.

Rector told me, "Private Mahone, you are the best recruit I have even seen in the Marine Corps boot camp training I will fight with you anywhere in the world." To the best of my recollection, Gunnery Sgt. Rector had served five tours in Vietnam as of 1969. I appreciated all the beating and stompings I experienced. They helped to make me a survivor and a leader.

I went on to graduate from other advanced trainings in the Marine Corps, and received orders for Vietnam in the winter 1969. I was ready for combat and wanted to do my part to stop the spread of Communism. Upon arriving in Vietnam, I was permanently stationed in An Hoa, Vietnam. I saw men die. I saw combat. I shot and killed a Vietcong. I was shot down from a helicopter on my way to the Red Betch Hospital. The chopper hobbled back to An Hoa, Vietnam, crippled from enemy gunfire. During the firefight, I blacked out from shock. Marine officers saved my life by shielding my body and protecting me from enemy gunfire.

I experienced a life-after-death experience when I blacked out from shock during enemy gunfire. I saw six angels that encircled me. They had a calming effect and I believed I was in Heaven. I awakened back in An Hoa, Vietnam. I feel as though I had died and lived to talk about it. I received an honorable discharge from the United States Marine Corps. I love the US Marines. Once a marine, always a marine. I was proud to have served.

US Special Police
Federal Protective Service
General Services Administration

It was a warm day when I was interviewed by administrators for the position of US Special Police, Federal Protective Service, General Services Administration during the summer of 1970. I was notified during the fall 1970, when I was 19, that I would be hired for the position because of my Marine Corps combat record and honorable discharge.

At the time, I was the youngest US Special Police, Federal Protective Service, General Services Administration, had ever hired at the time. I believe my starting salary was $4,500.00 per year; my duties were to provide security and protection for the US government buildings and employees against various terrorists, sabotage, and criminal acts; I assisted in investigations when criminal acts were perpetrated against federal installations and property. I was supervised by excellent administrators and supervisory police.

While on duty at the United States Customs House, I met District Director Heinz Hertz. As a result of placing a parking ticket on his vehicle for being illegally parked in the US Customs parking lot, and because of my honesty and zealousness, I was hired by the US Customs Service, U.S. Department of Treasury in late 1971. I was as an inspectional aide under the supervision of inspector John Rosania, at Midway Airport, in Chicago. As an inspectional aide I was a GS-4/5, initially earning approximately $5,200.00 per year. At Midway Airport, I was saddled with the responsibility of auditing inspector's manifests and duty entries. I was the point-of-contact person for banks, importers, carriers for interstate and intrastate commerce. At this post, I met a host of businessmen, bankers, truckers, cartmen, salesmen, and other international trade personnel.

Rosania, whom I loved dearly, came to be my "Godfather" at the US Customs Service.

He taught me everything that I knew about international traffic. He was a retired US Army sergeant or 20 years. John told me that the only way you could get promoted to inspector you must have a college degree. John had a type A personality. He was a natural leader; he was a perfectionist. He knew his job and vocation and was an inspectional troubleshooter. John bought me breakfast, lunch, dinner; he helped mold my behavior as a bureaucrat. John, along with inspector Jim Johnson, would help me with math. I was fortunate to be surrounded by such an elite, educated workforce. Other customs personnel were highly educated as well. Over time, I was promoted to inspectional aide, cashier, at O'Hare International Airport. Here, I was promoted to GS-6/7 making with overtime in excess of $30,000 per year in 1974. At this job, I was surrounded by personnel whom attended elite colleges and universities, the military, and other agencies such as the FBI, CIA, Secret Service, DEA, and other law enforcement agencies.

My primary duties in the inspectional services and finance, at the US Customs Service, US Department of Treasury, were to manage accounts receivable of over $500,000 per year from international passengers at O'Hare Airport, and audit import and export documents. As an inspectional aide, I met Muhammad Ali and Jesse Jackson; I came in contact with celebrities, shahs, sheiks, multimillionaires, kings, senators, congressmen, governors, and elected officials, as well as other dignitaries. On the down side, I also came into contact with drug traffickers and other criminals.

At the same time, I was married and studying for college courses four hours per day, all while working on the average of 13 hours per day during a seven-day week. Ron Zacck, a doctoral student in political science, was instrumental in helping me with political science.

There were but a handful of blacks working for the US Customs Service at O'Hare Airport during the 1970s, and the Civil Rights Movement was taking shape during this time. As such, even with a master's degree, I applied for more than 35 different jobs and was never promoted. I was suspended for no given reason. I became a union activist. I was outspoken. I was continuously audited by internal affairs. An employment strike seemed imminent. I was mocked, berated, and continuously talked with John Rosania. I finally became frustrated. I applied for the Bureau of Prisons, U.S. Department of Justice, to become employed as a correctional officer, GS-6. Even though this would mean a cut in salary. Prior to leaving the US Customs Service, Jack T. Lacy, regional commissioner, met with me and said, "You will do well, you are an ex-marine, a Vietnam combat veteran. Good Luck, Mel."

> Case Manager/Correctional Treatment
> Specialist/Correctional Officer
> US Bureau of Prisons, Department of Justice
> Milan FCI, MCC, Chicago
> 1977–1980

After working for other federal organizations, and as a result of being a bureaucrat, it came to pass that I assumed employment at Milan FCI, in Milan, Michigan, for the Federal Bureau of Prisons, U.S. Department of Justice as a correctional officer. As a correctional officer, I was assigned security and protection duties for inmates whom had violated federal statutes: people incarcerated who belonged to the mob, gang members, drug traffickers, kidnappers, extortionists, bank robbers, prostitutes, hijackers, terrorists, and political prisoners whom had and practiced a different ideology. I saved inmates lives on a regular basis; performed CPR on inmates at the institution. I escorted inmates to hospitals. I served and protected the community. I was also the victim of racism from inmates, as well as fellow staff members. I stayed focused and performed whatever duties my supervisors assigned to me.

When my daughter Angela was born, I transferred from the federal prison in Milan, Michigan, to the Metropolitan Correctional Center in Chicago, Illinois, where I was momentarily assigned to work as a correctional officer. This, however, was short-lived due to my suggesting the visiting rooms at the MCC Chicago be centralized. This suggestion set the stage for other architectural MCCs and community-based correctional facilities to follow suit. My suggestion saved the Federal Bureau of Prisons millions of dollars, man hours, improved the security, and the safety and orderly running of its main visiting rooms. Again, I took inmates to hospitals, funerals, and assisted in the security and running of the institution. As a result, I was promoted to case manager-correctional treatment specialist. I loved my new job. I was industrious and diligent. I treated all inmates firm but fair. My assigned duties were to provide counseling, advising, treatment, and referring and monitoring inmates' treatment progress. I also offered counseling for vocational skills, employment, drug and alcohol aftercare, parole, furlough, educational referral and institutional matters. I prepared weekly case management progress and classification reports; made regular court appearances for criminal and civil matters.

As time passed, I became the victim of excess stress while working on the average of 13 hours per day and attending college, along with raising a family. This began to take a toll on my mental and physical well-being. I was the victim of assaults and attempted murder on numerous occasions. On the job, I worked to prevent drugs from entering the institution and thwarted a sexual attack. As such, I became mentally fatigued, depressed, and slightly paranoid. Finally, the inevitable transpired, I was compelled to resign in September 1980.

Probation and Parole Officer
Florida Department of Corrections
Miami and Pensacola Florida

I was recruited and hired for the position by Evelyn Block and Tom Swenson. I had under my guardianship a host of committed criminals. Block was my immediate supervisor. I learned how to write pre-sentence investigations, post-sentence investigation reports, investigate criminal backgrounds, defend criminal cases in court, interrogate and interview criminal offenders. I performed my duties with zeal and diligence. I was highly motivated. I was very punctual.

One quiet evening, Tom Swenson, my supervisor for the main office at North Miami Beach, was spied upon and viciously gunned down by an alleged stalker. I left the office approximately 45 minutes before Tom was shot at least six times by the parolee. A crack investigative squad was assigned to the case, and gathered enough circumstantial evidence to charge the parolee with Tom's death. I took Tom's death very hard and requested to be transferred to Pensacola, Florida, where I stayed on the job for approximately three months before being reunited back with my wife and family in Chicago.

Training Specialist
Chicago City Colleges
Chicago, Illinois
1979–1988

As a training specialist for the Chicago City Colleges, I was committed to helping the "lost" young people of Chicago. These students were mostly young females who came from broken, dysfunctional, matriarchal-led families. Many of these students had poor study habits and were late to class on a regular basis. They had poor nutrition habits. Ninety percent of the young women were accepting state entitlements. They were not motivated. They had given up on life. Most of the women had poor life skills; some already the mother of at least two children. And most of their children were born out of wedlock. Most of the female students had low self-esteem. Seventy-five percent of the young women were of African-American descent.

    I had my hands full trying to provide quality education to these students. One young woman came to me and indicated that her relatives repeatedly told her that she would not ever amount to anything or have a life. She rebelled by dropping out of school and having children out of wedlock.

    I had to place all the students in groups when I taught them. I used the Lancasterian System, in which advanced students help teach less advanced ones. When I taught the group all of the students learned. When most of the women left my class, they passed the GED.

At Chicago City Colleges, I conducted orientation for incoming student and followed through conducting testing for program admissions, provide academic advice and counsel. I also assisted with conducting vocational counseling sessions, workshops and student recruitment, as well as intensive educational training and counseling in vocational sheltered workshops for the mentally ill in math, reading, English, and social studies.

During my enlightened tenure as a training specialist for the Chicago City Colleges, I felt a sense of accomplishment because most of the students that matriculated in my classes learned. They did everything in their power to move on to a higher level in life. Their self-esteem was elevated. Their behavior changed. They felt proud of themselves and became highly motivated. Some of the women demanded that their significant other provide support and psychological well-being. Most of the women went on to become nursing assistants, nurses, teaching aides; a few even matriculated in law school. Others went on with their lives and obtained professional employment. I inspired these women to find themselves. We won. I felt proud then and I feel proud today.

Employment Counselor
Mayor's Office of Employment and Training
Chicago, Illinois
Summers: 1984 and 1993

As an employment counselor for the Mayor's Office of Employment and Training in Chicago, I was involved in counseling wayward youths up to the age of 17. Most of these students were delinquent in some shape or form. Their families were broken and dysfunctional often, and the household was surviving on low incomes. The kids themselves lacked identity. Most were receiving entitlements.

I would send the youths to pre-determined city employment positions such as janitors, dishwashers, street cleaners, low-level city and county jobs that didn't require professional skills and where they could earn minimum wage. My main duties were impart youths with training orientation for assessment in vocational skills and employment projects, and also to provided them with employment counseling.

Educational Consultant
Educational Design Associates
Chicago
1988–1997

As a consultant, I offered advice to a multiplicity of government agencies in law enforcement on different topics that affected the quality of life to the world and the continental United States. Due to security reasons, I cannot and will not disseminate this information to the public about this job. However, the duties as assigned to me were to provide assessment of law enforcement data for various federal agencies and provide training and development services in staff development and stress management.

Parole Agent
Illinois Department of Corrections
Chicago
1985

I was "politically" referred to this position by a senior parole agent to work for Phil Mcgee, supervisory parole agent. When he interviewed me and hired me he said: "I hired you to fire you." In this position, as a Illinois parole agent, I carried a 357 Magnum, as this was a law enforcement position, and I was saddled with the responsibility of supervising mandatorily released convicted felons in the community after leaving prison. Most of these parolees were hardened criminals, some had, on the average, an eighth grade education, and they had lengthy criminal records. They lacked a positive employment record. The majority of them had never possessed a proven, lengthy employment record.

They came from dysfunctional families in the ghetto. Most were recidivists. When things seemed to moving in a positive direction, I soon found myself being constantly humiliated, degraded, and the victim of unfounded fault by supervisory Illinois state parole agent Phil Mcgee. On this job, I provided supervision of inmates and counseling for inmates. I referred inmates to education, employment, and substance abuse programs; and made regular court appearances for criminal and civil matters.

Public Safety Officer
Levy Security Consultants
Chicago
1991–1992

In this position, I provided security and helped protect commercial establishments and assets in downtown from theft, sabotage, terrorism, by providing public safety and security at the John Hancock Center, and the Marshall Fields department store. I furnished loss prevention services against theft and assisted in conducting criminal investigations.

Training Specialist
Harold Washington College, Chicago Police Academy
Chicago

At the Chicago Police Academy, my main responsibilities were to I educate and train Chicago police cadets, particularly in the area of responding to domestic disturbances throughout the city. I provided educational instruction to cadets and conducted communication, cultural diversity, and conflict management courses on domestic disturbances.

Residential Adviser/Case Manager
Salvation Army Community Correction Center
U.S. Department of Justice, Chicago
1997–1999

This was a federally contracted position in which I was saddled with the responsibility of providing case management services to recently released inmates from federal institutions throughout the United States. These residents consisted of inmates from federal institutions; I made cordial friends with many of the residents, as this was a community-based correctional facility. My duties, as assigned to me were, to managed activities and services for mentally ill residents, supply services on an assigned caseload, from onset to completion of the program; counsel residents regarding criminal justice issues and offer counseling on employment and vocational training.

Drug Counselor/Educator
Human Resource Development Institute
Chicago
2000–2001

As a drug counselor, I offered advice to a multiplicity of substance abusers from all stations in life. These were the forgotten people in our society. Most had lost hope and were merely surviving. Many were alcoholics and substance abusers who had hit rock bottom. My heart went out to them. I was assigned to counsel and educate parolees, probationers, senior citizens, and a number of other youths and adults who were struggling with addiction. I facilitated groups and educated offenders on substance abuse, conducted group sessions in nursing homes, training facilities, and in the Sheriff Day reporting program. I also counseled mentally ill clients, in which the *Diagnostic and Statistical Manual of Mental Disorders-IV* and American Society of Addiction Medicine assessment tools were used.

Social Services Career Trainee
Illinois Department of Human Services
Chicago
2001–2002

As a social service career trainee for the Illinois Department of Human Services, on the South Side of Chicago, I was referred to this position by Governor Ryan staff through Dan Profit. Because of political jealousies by the line staff, my salary was cut by 5 percent as I was hired at a higher salary range than other incoming staff at the same time. In this position, I met people mostly from the permanent underclass of the black community. The governor's staff wanted me to start as an administrator, but I opted to start as a line employee. As such, I counseled and provided services to public aid applicants coming through the intake department to determine their eligibility for food stamps, medical insurance, and other related services.

Substitute Teacher - Special Education
Chicago, Carmet City, Wilmette, and Skokie
1994–2004

As an educator and substitute schoolteacher for primary, middle schools, and secondary schools, I was had the responsibility of educating adolescents and youth throughout Cook County, Illinois. Some students came from good homes, some students were gifted. Others were deficient with the necessary knowledge to matriculate successfully through school as a result of their environment, family dynamics, and poor academic study habits. I helped as many students from all stages of learning as I could, imparting education to mentally ill and special needs students, and to those in general education in various subjects.

Consultant (Jail Division) and Technical Resource Provider
National Institute of Corrections, Longmont, Colorado
1995–1998

In the is position with a correctional facilities institution, I was on an on-call basis to provide training, development, education, vocational counseling, teaching, communication, and organization skills in correction and criminal justice.

Part-Time Investigator/Process Server
Luther Spencer and Associates Law Firm
Maywood, Illinois
1998–2000

My duties during this two-year stint were, but not limited too, investigating civil and criminal cases and processing subpoenas.

Mental Health Worker
Grand Prairie Services, Tinley Park, Illinois
2001–2003

My duties here were to offer counseling to mental health clients. I also dispensed medications, provided transportation, and prepared case management reports on each client in respect to their progress in a community living arrangement.

Professor of Criminal Justice
Harold Washington College, Chicago Police Academy
Chicago
1995–1997

One of my first jobs as an instructor was to teach criminal justice courses to undergraduate and graduate students at Harold Washington College, Chicago Police Academy, where I also developed course curriculums and devised challenging assignments for students; reviewed and counseled students regarding career planning options; and assisted in managing and giving advise to faculty. I then continued to teach criminal justice at several colleges and universities in Illinois. During my career as a professor, I have worked at Chicago State University, Chicago, 1997–2008; Columbia College, Elgin, 2004; Loyola University at Chicago, 2004; Westwood College at Carmet City, and Woodridge, and O'Hare Airport and Downtown College, 2004–2005, 2008; Governors State University, University Park, 2003–2005. In 2009, I taught criminal justice courses at Brown-Mackie College, in Michigan City, Indiana.

I worked as a professor and coordinator of the criminal justice department at Olympic College, Bremerton, Washington, from 2005 to 2007, where I managed assigned classrooms, planned, organized, directed, coordinated, and re-wrote the entire criminal justice curriculum for the school. I served on Olympic college's criminal justice advisory committee and rewrote the entire criminal justice curriculum in 2006. I also conducted testing for academic appropriateness and orientation for incoming students.

I was employed as an online facilitator at Aspen University, Denver, Colorado, from 2008 to 2009, where I taught and facilitated online criminal justice courses and audited students' course curriculums. As dean of Criminal Justice and Security Administration at Taylor Business Institute in Chicago, from 2008 to 2009, I had a trio of responsibilities at this small, private college: managed the criminal justice department; conducted academic testing as well as advised, counseled, and assisted in the registration of incoming students; and supervised a multiplicity of faculty from various departments in carrying out their academic duties. I also performed other duties as assigned by the president and ministerial departments.

My Academic Career

Education has always been important to me. After returning from Vietnam and working for several federal agencies, I was determined to attend college and learn as much as I could in areas where I believed my learned skills, knowledge, along with my personal goals of helping others would be better served. I received Bachelor's of Science degree in sociology and individualized curriculums in 1975 from Chicago State University, Chicago, Illinois. I earned my Master's of Science degree in corrections in 1977, from Chicago State University; obtained a Ph.D. in criminal justice with a special emphasis in corrections from Union Institute and University, Cincinnati, Ohio, in 2002. I completed postgraduate credit semester hours beyond a master's degree in management, personnel administration, industrial relations, organizational development, informational systems, history, criminal justice and corrections, public administration, training and development, curriculum and instruction, training, business law, and paralegalism for an approximate total of sixty (60) credits beyond a master's degree at Roosevelt and Chicago State Universities.

Recognition

In 1997, I was listed in the International *Who's Who of Professionals* for lifetime accomplishments. I received an honorable mention for honesty from US Customs Service, Department of Treasury. I received the following suggestion awards: Pistol Range Safety at US Customs House, 610 S. Canal St., Chicago, Illinois (1971). US Bureau of Prisons, US Department of Justice, Chicago, Illinois (1979) suggestion award for decentralizing visiting rooms (Honorable Mention). I scored the highest overall score/percentile of 90 percent out of 100 percent, in a class of 30 while at the National Training Academy, United States Penitentiary Atlanta Bureau of Prisons, United States Department of Justice (1978), for Correctional Officers.

In 1969, United States Marine Corps, Boot Camp, San Diego, California, Platoon 1138, Honor Platoon. Received Vietnam combat service ribbon, National Defense service ribbon, and good conduct ribbon. Honorably discharged United States Marine Corps, 1970.

Employee of the "Month" Salvation Army under contract with the Bureau of Prisons, United States Department of Justice, 1998.

Criminal Justice Affiliations

American Correctional Association
National Institute of Corrections
American Society of Criminal Justice
John Howard Association
American Society of Criminology

Criminal Justice Courses and General Education Courses Taught

Management and Supervision in Law Enforcement
Police Community Relations
Race, Crime and Violence
Research Methods for Criminology and Criminal Justice
White Collar
Criminology I
Criminology II
Introduction to Criminal Justice
Introduction to Investigation
Professional Responsibilities in Criminal Justice Ethics
Criminal Law
Probation and Parole
Adult Institutions
Community-Based Corrections
Stress Classes
Criminal Law II

Terrorism
Introduction to Corrections
Police Management
Report Writing
English
Correction Law
Critical Issues in Juvenile Delinquency
Critical Issues in Criminal Justice
Junior Seminar
Corrections I
Corrections II
Administration and Justice
Criminal Justice and Public Policy
Basic Security Concepts and Practices
Constitutional Law
Electronic Security and Surveillance
Firearms Safety and Security
Criminal Investigations
Defensive Tactics and Law Enforcement Seminar
Homeland Security and Terrorism
Intro to Law Enforcement
Criminal Procedure
Technology in Law Enforcement
Public Policy (Criminal Justice)
General Education Courses: English, Reading, Science, Math, Civics, US Constitution, Social Studies, and History.

Extracurricular Activities

From 2004 to 2005, I served to the vice president for "Energy," which assisted poverty stricken youths in Chicago. My duties included fundraised and assisting in the every day running of organizational tasks. I assisted in writing grants for Energy, requesting grant money from the federal government in the millions of dollars for projects for youth.

I served on the board of directors for the YMCA in Bremerton, Washington (2007–2008), assisting in planning, organizing, directing, and coordinating various tasks on a daily basis.

Attended various criminal justice conferences and served on panels for the betterment of research and policymaking all over the country (2005–2007).

I served on the board of directors with the Safer Foundation in Chicago, Illinois, in 2009. As a board member, I ensured that there were an adequate number of educational specialist teaching general educational development courses at Cook County Jail and other security settings where inmates are housed. I also ensured that there was appropriate curriculum content and other educational materials readily available for professional staff to use in providing the appropriate education to incarcerated inmates. The educational staff was exclusively volunteers from the private sector.

In 2009, I served as chairman for "professional growth" on the Taylor Business Institute's self-study for the Accrediting Council for Independent Colleges and Schools. I was also as chairman of Criminal Justice Advisory Committee at Taylor Business Institute in Chicago, in 2009. I was also became chairman of serving learning in 2009: service learning at Taylor Business Institute is defined as a teaching method that enriches learning by empowering students through meaningful service that benefit the common good, expressing the concerns of the communities from which Taylor Business Institute students come. Service learning must be coordinated and structured by the college. It is an activity that is integrated into influencing the lifelong learning of Taylor Business Institute's students. Service learning must have a component and an articulated learning outcome. Under the criminal justice and security administration curriculum, terrorism is the course that service learning was to be used by the institute. I was also an adviser on the advisory board for Taylor Business Institute in nominating our "Best Students" to the Alpha Beta Kappa National Honor

Society (2009–present). At Taylor, I was also on the institute's building safety committee, which is responsible for ensuring that the campus grounds for students and faculty are safe and secure on a regular basis (2009).

While at TBI, I attended a workshop on "Understanding and Undergirding the Underserved," which was given by Kimberly D. Thomas, clinical professor of law at the University of Michigan Law School and co-founder of the Juvenile Justice Clinic. This workshop, held at the Taylor Business Institute in May 2009, gave reflections on different learning styles, motivation of students, cultural diversity, and the underserved student.

In 2002, I wrote an unpublished Ph.D. dissertation, which is in Library of Congress at the Union Institute and University titled "What Are the Economic Feasibility and Social Impacts on Privatized Prisons in America?" I've served on the doctoral committee at Union Institute & University (2002–2005).

Chapter

8

Final Observations

In an article by Stephen Losey for the *Federal Times* a study showed that the federal government employed more Hispanic people in 2008 than in any other year, but the Equal Employment Opportunity Commission says much more work still needs to be done. The article states: "The Office of Personnel Management publicly released a report January 15 that said 8 percent of the federal work force was Hispanic in fiscal 2008. That's up from 6.4 percent in fiscal 1998, and 2.9 percent in 1972."

The Homeland Security Department, EEOC and Social Security Administration showed some of the biggest percentage increases in Hispanic employment in 2008, OPM said.

But EEOC released its own report Jan 14 that said Hispanic federal employees feel they are discriminated against and are not advancing in their careers.

An article by (Castelli, 2009) stated that the Obama Administration last week launched a new program to boost veteran hiring at all agencies.

The plan calls for setting up new teams at each department to promote veterans hiring, train hiring staffs to better assist vets applying for jobs, and track progress.

Obama officials say there are no specific hiring targets. All the agencies have to show is that more vets are employed by veterans day next year.

"It's a very simple metric.... That is our base and our goal is that every one of those [agency-by-agency veteran employment] numbers increases," a year now, said federal personnel director John Berry at a Nov. 12 news conference.

John Wilson, an assistant national legislative director at Disabled American Veterans, said the government's complex hiring system could be the main barrier to increasing the number of veteran hires. "You apply for a job—that takes several months—then it takes four to six months after that to learn whether or not you've been hired," he said. Without overall hiring reforms, Wilson said he's not "optimistic that we're going to have any significant change."

Still, Wilson applauded the administration's focus on increasing veterans hiring. He said the focus should be on those agencies with comparably low veterans hiring levels and on increasing outreach to disabled veterans, where hiring rates remain low.

To help agencies along, President Barack Obama last week signed an executive order creating a new program called the Veterans Employment Initiative. It requires agencies to:

- Develop a plan to promote employment opportunities for veterans.
- Establish a Veterans Employment Program Office to develop and carry out the plan within 120 days of the order.

- Provide annual training for human resources managers to ensure they're giving veterans preference and are exercising special hiring authorities for veterans.

To oversee the initiative, Obama also established an interagency Council on Veterans Employment led by the labor and Veterans affairs departments and the Office of Personnel Management. The council will:

- Coordinate government wide recruitment and training to increase the number of veterans agencies employ.
- Serve as a forum for promoting employment opportunities to veterans.
- Establish way to measure the effectiveness of the initiative.

The existing veterans preferences provide former service members extra points on their federal employment applications, boosting their chances of being hired. "The past system was based on...'here is your five points, here is your 10 points. Good luck,' "Berry said. "That was quite frankly, in my opinion, not enough."

In September, the Labor Department reported that 11.3 percent of veterans returning from Iraq and Afghanistan are unemployed, higher than the 10 percent jobless rate nationwide.

Men and women returning from Iraq "have the highest unemployment rate ever of any veterans group and community," Berry said. "We need to go above and beyond not only for them but all vets, but this program will begin...with a heavy focus and emphasis on those folks returning right now into this environment."

The new executive order preserves all existing preference programs and sets up new Veterans Employment Program Offices—at every agency and OPM. These staff will act as head hunters: asking veterans what their interests, skills and long-term goals are; then, helping them navigate the federal hiring process to find appropriate jobs, Berry said.

These offices will broaden the network of assistance available to veterans through the Transition Assistance Program (TAP) run by the Defense, Veterans Affairs, Transportation and Labor departments, said Ray Jefferson, assistant Labor secretary for Veterans Employment and Training Services. TAP provides résumé building and other career development services to help veterans and retiring service members translate their military skills to civilian jobs in the public and private sectors.

Under the New Veterans Employment initiative, TAP will not only provide assistance to service members, but also train human resource professionals and employment counselors on the federal hiring process, veterans preferences and streamlined hiring authorities, Jefferson said.

When exercising the streamlined hiring authorities, agencies must adhere to merit hiring principles in determining the best-qualified candidate for a job, Berry said.

The Homeland Security Department is ahead of the game in carrying out the Veterans Employment Initiative, Berry said.

Homeland Security has efforts underway to grow its veteran ranks from 46,000 to 50,000 by 2012, said Jeffrey Neal, the department's chief human capital officer. The department also hired a full-time veteran employment coordinator and has plans to hire another full-time coordinator at headquarters and three full-time coordinators to manage veterans hiring at its three largest components, Neal said.

Veterans are ideal job candidates for Homeland Security positions because they've already proven they're capable of handling complex security tasks in their military careers, Neal said. In addition, many recently discharged service members have security clearances, which are key for Homeland Security jobs, Neal said. And they can be hired quickly through myriad streamlined hiring authorities, such as preferential hiring for service disabled veterans, he said.

"There are not a lot of excuses not to hire a veteran," Neil said.

Although DHS has taken many of the actions outlined in the Nov.9 executive order, Neal said the order is an important document that will further highlight the importance of hiring veterans at DHS.

"When you have the president of the United States saying, 'I want something done,' and the secretary of Homeland Security saying, 'I want something done,' the people in leadership positions in the department...are going to listen to those leaders and do what they're asked to do," Neil said.

A recent news story in *USA Today* (Cauchon, 2010), suggests that federal employees earn higher average salaries than private-sector workers in more than eight out of 10 occupations. "Accountants, nurses, chemists, surveyors, cooks, clerks and janitors are among the wide range of jobs that get paid more on average in the federal government than in the private sector," the article reported.

Overall, federal workers earned an average salary of $67,691 in 2008 for occupations that exist both in government and in the private sector, according to Bureau of Labor Statistics data. The average pay for the same mix of jobs in the private sector was $60,046 in 2008, the most recent data available.

These salary figures do not include the value of health, pension and other benefits, which averaged $40,785 per federal employee in 2008 versus $9,882 per private worker, according to the Bureau of Economic Analysis.

Federal pay has become a hot political issue in recent months because of concerns over the federal budget deficit and recession-battered wages in the private sector.

Sen. Scott Brown, R.-Mass., made federal pay an issue in his successful campaign to fill Edward Kennedy's seat and is fighting for a pay freeze.

The federal government spends about $125 billion annually on compensation for about twp million civilian employees. "The data flip the conventional wisdom on its head," says Cato Institute budget analyst Chris Edwards, a critic of federal pay policy. "Federal workers make substantially more than private workers, not less, in addition to having a large advantage in benefits."

But National Treasury Employees Union President Colleen Kelly says, "The comparison is faulty because it 'compares apples and oranges.' Federal accountants, for example, perform work that has more complexity and requires more skill than accounting work in the private sector," she says.

"When you look at the actual duties, you see that very few federal jobs align with those in the private sector," she says. She says federal employees are paid an average of 26 percent less than non-federal workers doing comparable work.

176   Coping With Stress and Building Leadership

Office of Personnel Management spokeswoman Sedelta Verble says higher pay also reflects the longevity and older age of federal workers.

USA Today used Bureau of Labors Statistics (BLS) data to compare salaries in every federal job that had a private sector equivalent. For example, the federal government's 57,000 registered nurses—working for the Veterans Affairs and elsewhere—were paid an the average of $74,460 a year, $10,680 more than the average for private-sector nurses.

The BLS reports that 216 occupations covering 1.1 million federal workers exist in both the federal government and the private sector. An additional 124 federal occupations covering 750,000 employees—air-traffic controllers, tax collectors and others—did not have direct equivalents, according to the BLS.

Federal jobs have more limited salary ranges than private-sector jobs, some of which have million-dollar payouts.

Key findings:

- **Federal.** The federal pay premium cut across all job categories—white collar, blue collar, management, professional, technical and low-skill. In all, 180 jobs paid better average salaries in the federal government; 36 paid better in the private sector.
- **Private.** The private sector paid more on average in a select group of high-skill occupations, including lawyers, veterinarians, and airline pilots. The government's 5,200 computer research scientists made an average of $95,190, about $10,000 less than average in the corporate world.
- **State and Local.** State government employees had an average salary of $47,231 in 2008, about 5 percent less than comparable jobs in the

private sector. City and county workers earned an average of $43,589, about 2 percent more than private workers in similar jobs. State and local workers have higher total compensation than private workers when the value of benefits is included.

Job comparisons

Average federal salaries exceed average private-sector pay in 83 percent of comparable occupations. A sampling of average annual salaries in 2008, the most recent data available:

Job	Federal	Private	Difference
Airline pilot, flight engineer	$93,690	$120,012	-$26,322
Broadcast technician	$90,310	$49,265	$41,045
Budget analyst	$73,140	$65,532	$7,608
Chemist	$98,060	$72,120	$25,940
Civil engineer	$85,970	$76,184	$9,786
Clergy member	$70,460	$39,247	$31,213
Computer, information Systems manager	$122,020	$115,705	$6,315
Computer support specialist	$45,830	$54,875	-$9,045
Cook	$38,400	$23,279	$15,121
Crane, tower operator	$54,900	$44,044	$10,856
Dental assistant	$36,170	$32,069	$4,101
Economist	$101,020	$91,065	$9,965
Editor	$42,210	$54,803	-$12,593
Electrical engineer	$86,400	$84,653	$1,747
Financial analyst	$87,400	$81,232	$6,168
Graphic Designer	$70,820	$46,565	$24,255

Job	Federal	Private	Difference
Highway maintenance worker	$42,720	$31,376	$11,344
Janitor	$30,110	$24,188	$ 5,922
Landscape architect	$80,830	$58,380	$ 22,450
Laundry-dry-cleaning	$33,100	$19,945	$13,155
Lawyer	$123,660	$126,763	-$3,103
Librarian	$76,110	$ 63,284	$12,826
Locomotive engineer	$48,440	$63,125	-$14,685
Machinist	$51,530	$44,315	$7,215
Mechanical engineer	$ 88,690	$77,554	$11,136
Office clerk	$34,260	$29,863	$4,397
Optometrist	$61,530	$106,665	-$45,135
Paralegal	$60,340	$48,890	$11,450
Pest control worker	$48,670	$33,657	$14,995
Physician, surgeon	$176,050	$177,102	-$1,052
Physician assistant	$77,770	$87,783	-$10,013
Procurement clerk	$40,640	$34,082	$6,558
Public relations manager	$132,410	$88,241	$44,169
Recreation worker	$43,630	$21,671	$21,959
Registered nurse	$74,460	$63,780	$10,680
Respiratory therapist	$46,740	$50,443	-$3,703
Secretary	$44,500	$33,829	$10,671
Sheet metal worker	$49,700	$43,725	$5,975
Statistician	$88,520	$78,065	$10,455
Surveyor	$78,710	$67,336	$11,374

Source: Bureau of Labor Statistics, USA Today analysis

Epilogue

It was a hot, humid day of July 2010, when I arrived in Lexington, Kentucky. This city has gone through a major transformation in size of population and its economic base since World War II. I looked for employment everyday until the University of Kentucky, Chandler Hospital, called me to work on their security staff. I was told that I was overqualified, as I possessed a Ph.D. in criminal justice and corrections. I had also worked in every area of the criminal justice system as a police officer, correctional officer, parole agent, and probation officer.

The line staff wanted to know why a person with my background wanted to be a security officer? I told them repeatedly that it was my desire to become an adjunct criminal justice professor and then an assistant criminal justice professor in Kentucky. It was not long ago afterward that I was called to be an adjunct professor at Sullivan University, in Louisville. And then I was called to be an assistant professor for University of the Cumberlands, in Williamsburg, commencing August 1, 2011. I am thankful to have been called for these positions, as I was overqualified for the security officer position.

Stress and FCI, Milan, Michigan

It was cold, snowy, and gloomy day in Milan, Michigan, when I started my career in corrections as a correctional officer in December 1977, for the Bureau of Prisons, United States Department of Justice. I lived at the correctional institution in the bachelors officers quarters. My first assignment was patrolling the yard on day duty, from 8 a.m. until 4 p.m. I had to walk in 10 inches of snow, patrolling the yard for the safety and orderliness at the institution. Because I was living in the bachelors officers quarters, I was the first person management called for an assignment when another correctional officer was absent. I worked at least three to four days in overtime on a regular basis, during a two-week pay period. I worked critical posts, such as yard, segregation, tower, food service, hall, and dormitory duty.

Yard duty meant walking all over the yard inside the institution to protect inmates from fighting or doing anything illegal while they were outside. Segregation detail was hazardous and dangerous to me because I had to stop fights when inmates were fighting with knives and other homemade weapons. Inmates in segregation were the most dangerous ones; they had been sent for protection, discipline, or waiting to be transferred to another institution in the federal prison system.

Tower duty was long arduous, hours, working until midnight during the winter. The tower was cold and dark. I had to move a light beam lamp from one spot to the other, looking for inmates who might try to escape from the roof or through the yard on the ground through meshed, looped wire that was laid on the top and bottom and top of the fences and stretched around the perimeter of the institution. I had to be ready with the light beam lamp, watching out and looking for an inmate who tried to escape. I was armed in the tower with a sawed-off shotgun and other weapons in the case of an attempted escape. I had authorization from management to "shoot to kill."

Food service duty was critical to the orderly running of the institution, as well. I had to stand guard at my post while hundreds of inmates passed a food line and were rationed food. They then sat down one by one at different tables to eat. If an argument broke out, it was my responsibility to press my body alarm and send for other correctional officers at the institution for assistance. It was always very tense standing guard in the cafeteria. One could ever tell when an argument or a fight would disrupt.

Hall duty was the safest duty of all. I had to keep a watch out if inmates were fighting or moving contraband through the halls at the institution. Dormitory duty was the most hazardous duty because I had to be vigilant against heated arguments and fights, contraband being passed between inmate, and inmates consuming drugs in the washrooms. I was completely unarmed when I watched inmates in the dormitory. There were about 100 inmates per dormitory, and I was assigned to guard one dormitory of inmates every 90 days.

It was not the inmates, however, who caused problems for me at the institution. The problems were with the staff and the interpersonal relationships I had with management at FCI Milan. I was told on more than one occasion various staff were envious of me because of my background; the fact that I had a master's degree and the other correctional officers did not have my overall experience. Once my one-year of probation was over, I would pose a threat to the other officers who were eligible for promotions to various other positions throughout the institution and the country as well. I was treated differently by management and line staff because of my overall background and experiences. I never told anyone or said anything to the warden, and he said to me, "Mahone, you can take your master's degree and put it in your back pocket." His supervisors condoned the unjustifiable treatment toward me by fellow officers. They, along with line and staff workers, would find unwarranted fault in my work. Correctional officers would entertain the hearsay from fellow coworkers and inmates. I would spend a lot of productive time responding to outlandish gossip and hearsay by staff, management, and inmates. I was constantly defending my character and work ethic. I was working overtime, working difficult posts, defending myself against the gossip and rumors. As a result, I was stressed and burned out. I suffered from post-traumatic stress disorder (PTSD) and depression. To cope with the stress, I stopped working overtime and changed my employment from corrections to education.

In 1977 when, I was on "probation" as a correctional officer at FCI Milan, Michigan, at least 20 different correctional officers resigned from their positions. For the most part, they resigned because of low salaries, lack of support by management, and the stress, which led to burnout. To handle their stress and come to grips with burnout, many correctional workers turned to alcohol, prescription drugs, or illicit drugs as a coping mechanism. Many of them came into conflict with their significant others as well. There was a need to have programs in the federal prison system to help correctional workers who were burnt out and suffering from stress. Due to budget restrictions at the time that I resigned from the "Bureau," these programs were not in place in 1980 at the Metropolitan Correctional Center in Chicago, Illinois.

I changed jobs only to discover that stress in primary-school education was more stressful than in law enforcement and corrections. I was charged with teaching primary-school children in the place of their regular teacher. I was a substitute schoolteacher. Helping grade-school children whom have not reached the mental age of maturity is very difficult. Children act out without knowing it. You give some of these children educational tasks and they don't fully comprehend the simple tasks they were assigned. They act out without being fully aware it. They believe that it is fun time when a substitute teacher is providing them instruction. Children don't respect substitute teachers. In their immature minds, they think it is "time out "when a substitute teacher gives them assignments. I counted how many times that I had to tell a student, "Please stop and be quiet." It seemed as if I had made that statement at least 30 times in one hour, and stopping to do so took up much and sometimes all the time that I needed to teach. I was mentally exhausted when I would come home from teaching for several years. Grade-school education aggravated my stress and depression condition. I was a substitute educator for 10 years.

Upon leaving teaching primary education, I started teaching adults. I taught criminal justice to older students, teachers, police officers, managers, and correctional officers. Teaching adults taught me how to cope with stress. I taught in an environment that made me feel good; and I was not mentally exhausted when I came home from work every night. I taught on the average of 12 to 15 hours a week. I did what made me feel good. I was an educator. I coped with stress by learning breathing exercises, taking warm baths, making love, taking brisk one-mile walks, watching public TV and nonviolent movies, avoiding caffeine, sticking to low fat, low pork diet, meditating, and doing light exercises

What is stress? Stress is a generic term that can include a variety of feelings: worrying, anxiety, tension, depression, anger, fear, and fatigue. The body's response to stress is meant to protect and support us. Our body automatically goes into overdrive, engaging the stress response. Most modern stresses, however, do not call for flight or fight. Our experience of stress is generally related to how we respond to an event, not to the event itself.

Stress is a natural bodily response and it is not always bad. A moderate level of stress can actually help performance by enhancing motivation and heightening our senses. Acute stress results from demands and pressures of the recent past and anticipated demands and pressures of the near future. Episodic acute stress makes your life feel disorderly, in perpetual crisis, or out of control. Chronic stress is unrelenting demands and pressures for indefinite periods of time. Chronic stress is stress that wears you down day after day and seems endless. Symptoms of stress are sleep disturbances, back, shoulder or neck pain, tension or migraine headaches, upset or acid stomach, cramps, heartburn, irregular heartbeat, palpitations, asthma or shortness of breath, chest pain, increased use of drugs, alcohol, and tobacco. [16].

To reduce stress one should meditate, use the time for each task effectively, delegate, allow extra time, sauna, exercises, utilize muscle relaxation. Always have time out, adjust your work schedule to combat against unneeded stress by working fewer hours, take vacations, relax, and have timeouts. And listen to soothing music with a healthy diet.

10 Best Leadership Qualities

The ideal leader has a mission. He knows what to do in an organization and how to do it. The ideal leader has a vision. He prognosticates what will transpire within 10 years from the present. The ideal leader knows how to communicate in different cultures and with people of various ethnicities verbally as well as in writing. The ideal leader supports and leads his subordinates. He gives orders and takes them, he gives constructive criticism to his unit of command. The ideal leader believes in himself by being self-confident. He learns from other people. He trusts people. He is highly motivated. The ideal leader continuously presents a positive attitude toward his subordinates in the organization. The ideal leader manages his subordinates by being seen intermittently during peak hours of the day yet keeping careful vigil over his subordinates. He gives positive strokes to his unit of command. The ideal leader has integrity. He is open-minded and sincere. He is empathetic toward his subordinates. The ideal leader manages to adjust differently to various subordinates in the organization because they learn differently under his management and leadership style. No subordinate is the same. The ideal leader shares his successes with his subordinates by motivating them when there are positive outcomes.

Leadership Defined

Leadership reflects definitions from all walks of life, management, politicians, statesman, and educators, etc. A dictionary definition: Function: noun 1: the office of position of a leader; 2: capacity to lead; 3: the act or an instance of leading-—Source: Merriam-Webster online.[17]

Here are a few other definitions:

1. "My definition of a leader...is a man who can persuade people to do what they don't want to do, or do what they're too lazy to do, and like it."
 —Harry S. Truman (1884–1972), 33rd US President

2. "You cannot manage men into battle. You manage things; you lead people."
 —Grace Hopper, Admiral, US Navy

3. "Leadership is a two-way street, loyalty up and loyalty down. Respect for one's superiors; care for one's crew."
 —Grace Hopper, Admiral, US Navy

4. "The first job of a leader is to define a vision for the organization...Leadership of the capacity to translate vision into reality."
 —Warren Bennis, President, University of Cincinnati

5. "The ultimate test of practical leadership is the realization of intended, real change that meets people's enduring needs."
 —James MacGregor Burns, authority on leadership studies

6. "Managers have subordinates—leaders have followers."
 —Murray Johannsen, entrepreneur, speaker, and corporate trainer

7. "If your actions inspire others to dream more, learn more, do more and become more, you are a leader."
 —John Quincy Adams (1767– 1848), 6th US President

8. "I am looking for a lot of men who have an infinite capacity to not know what can't be done."
 —Henry Ford, industrialist, founder of Ford Motor Corp.

9. "As for the best leaders, the people do not notice their existence. The next best, the people honor and praise. The next, the people fear, the next, the people hate."
—Lao Tse (604-531 B.C.), Chinese philosopher and founder of Taoism

10. "A manager takes people where they want to go. A great leader takes people where they don't necessarily want to go but ought to."
—Rosalynn Carter, former First Lady

Leadership and Me

As a correctional treatment specialist, assistant criminal justice professor, and dean of criminal justice and security administration, I was a leader and a manager. I skillfully supervised and managed. That is what a leader does: he supervises and manages his subordinates. It all depends on the leader's leadership style as to the way he provides leadership.

My style of leadership and management is democratic. Why? Because all subordinates learn differently. Basically, leadership and management goes hand and hand, and a leader manages by example for others to follow. Management entails meeting objectives in a sufficient manner. Basically, leadership and management is a lifelong learning experience which involves traditional versus progressive leadership education. Traditional is static. Progressive is dynamic. Static remains the same. There is no progress. Dynamic is ever-changing. There is progress.

Leadership and management have subordinates who all learn in different ways. Learning is an enduring change of behavior in respect to leadership and management. If behavior is static, no leadership or management takes place. If leadership and management are progressive then learning takes place. Therefore, in my mind, here are the underpinnings of the philosophy of leadership and management :

- Each employee is different.
- Therefore, each employee has to be managed differently.
- The manager must adjust his management and leadership style abilities to each and every employee's learning ability.
- The manager should be empathetic based on the employee's subordinate learning ability.
- The manager should be firm but fair for each employee to learn.
- The manager leader when training employees should use a Lancasterian method of grouping for the most optimum means of teaching many in a captive audience, distant learning, or chat room electronically.

As a correctional treatment specialist, I successfully led and managed 80 inmates under my unit of command. As an assistant criminal justice professor, I successfully taught, managed and led thousands of students under my unit of command over the past two decades. As dean of criminal justice and security administration, I successfully led, managed, and instructed employees in all criminal justice departments at various colleges and universities.

Notes

1. Breakthough Collaborative, http://breakthroughcollaborative.org/
2. "Drowned Boys Case Takes Toll on Officers, Clergy," *Florida Times Union* (Jacksonville), November 10, 1994, A6.
3. "On-the-Job Stress in Policing: Reducing It, Preventing It," *National Institute of Justice Journal,* January 2000, 18-24.
4. "Stress on the Job," *Newsweek,* April 25, 1988, 43.
5. "On-the-Job Stress in Policing: Reducing It, Preventing It," *National Institute of Justice Journal,* January 2000, 18-24.
6. Kevin Barrett, "Police Suicide: Is Anyone listening?" *Journal of Safe Management of Disruptive and Assault Behavior,* Spring 1997, 6-9.
7. Ibid.
8. Robin N Haarr and Merry Morash, "Coping Strategies Among Police Officers," "Gender, Race and strategies of Coping with Occupational Stress in Policing," *Justice Quarterly,* Vol. 16, No. 2, June 1999, 303-336.
9. Mark H. Hansel, "A Conceptual Model and Implications for Coping with Stressful Events in Police Work," *Criminal Justice and Behavior* Vol. 27, No. 3, 2000, 375.
10. Ibid.
11. "On-the-Job Stress in Policing," p.20
12. Bryan Vila, "Tired Cops: Probable Connections Between Fatigue and the Performance, Health, and Safety of Patrol Officers," *American Journal of Police,* Vol. 15, No. 2, 1996, 51-92.
13. Bryan Vila, et al; *Evaluating the Effects of Fatigue on Police Patrol Officers: Final Report,* Washington D.C.: National Institute of Justice, 2000.

14. Bryan Vila and Dennis Jay Kenney, "Tired Cops: The Prevalence and Potential Consequences of Police Fatigue," *NIJ Journal*, No 248, 2002,19

15. Bryan Vila, and Erik Y. Taiji, "Fatigue and Police Officer Performance," Paper presented at the annual meeting of the American Society of Criminology, Chicago, 1996.

16. University of Maryland Medical Center, www.umm.edu/patiented/articles/what biological_effects_of_acute_stress,_000031_2.htm.

17. Legacee, http://www.legacee.com/Info/Leadership/Definitions.html

Bibliography

Allen, James. *As a Man Thinketh*. Thrifty Books, 2009.

Barlow, David H. *Clinical Handbook of Psychological Disorders: A Step-by-Step Treatment Manual* (3rd ed.). New York: The Guilford Press, 2001.

Brady, Joseph V. "Ulcers in Executive Monkeys." *Scientific American* 199. (1958): 89-95

Bruhn, John G., and Stewart Wolf. *The Roseto Story: An Anatomy of Health*. Norman: University of Oklahoma Press, 2003.

Castelli, Elise. "Managers Pressured to Hire More Vets." *Federal Times,* November 16, 2009

Cauchon, Dennis. "It Pays to Work for Uncle Sam." *USA Today*, March 5, 2010.

Cox, Tom. *Stress*. London: Palgrave, 1978.

Drucker, Peter F. *Management: Tasks, Responsibilities, Practices*. New York: Harper & Row, 1974.

Giuliani, Rudolph W. *Leadership*. New York: Hyperion, 2002

Goodfield, June. "Humanity in Science: A Perspective and a Plea." *Science* 198 (1977): 580-585.

Hagerlof, H. "Psychophysiological Reactions During Emotion Stress." *Emotional Stress: Physiological and Psychological*

Reactions, Medical, Industrial, and Military Implications. Ed. Lennart Levi. New York: American Elsevier Publishing Co.

Han, Peter. *Nobodies to Somebodies: How 100 Leaders in Business, Politics, Arts, Science, and Nonprofits Got Started.* New York: Penguin Group/Portfolio Trade, 2006.

Hierstetter, Brad. "The Motivated Project Team." Defense AT&L. 38, no.7 (1997): 56–59.

Hill, Napoleon. *The Law of Success in Sixteen Lessons.* New York: Snow Ball Publishing, 2009.

Hill, Napoleon. *Napoleon Hill's Golden Rules: The Lost Writings.* Hoboken: John Wiley & Sons, Inc., 2008.

Hill, Napoleon and W. Clement Stone. *Success Through a Positive Mental Attitude.* New York: Pocket Books, 2007.

Hill, Napoleon. *Think and Grow Rich.* Tribeca Books, 2010.

Ivancevich, John M., and Michael T. Matteson. *Controlling Work Stress: Effective Human Resource and Management Strategies.* San Francisco: Jossey-Bass, 1989.

Ivancevich, John M., and Michael T. Matteson. *Managing Job Stress and Health: The Intelligent Person's Guide.* New York: Free Press, 1982.

Ivancevich, John M., and Michael T. Matteson. *Stress and Work: A Managerial Perspective.* Illinois: Scott Foresman and Co., 1980.

Kimbro, Dennis and Napoleon Hill. *Think and Grow Rich: A Black Choice.* New York: Ballantine Books, 1997.

Losey, Stephen. "Hispanic Hiring Gains-with Qualifications." *Federal Times*, January 19, 2009.

Lowe, Tamara. *Get Motivated!: Overcome Any Obstacle, Achieve Any Goal, and Accelerate Your Success with*

Motivational DNA. New York: Crown Business/Doubleday Publishing Group, 2009.

McCoy, Thomas J. *Compensation and Motivation: Maximizing Employee Performance with Behavior-Based Incentive Plans.* New York: AMACON Books, 1992.

Pelletier, Kenneth. *Holistic Medicine: From Stress to Optimum Health.* New York: Delacorte Press, 1979.

Quick, Thomas L. *The Manager's Motivation Desk Book.* Hoboken: John Wiley & Sons, 1985.

Schwab, Robert S. and John S. Prichard. "Situational Stresses and Extrapyramidal Disease in Different Personalities." *Life Stress and Bodily Disease: Proceedings of the Association for Research in Nervous Mental Diseases.* Baltimore: Williams & Wilkins, 1950

Selye, Hans. *The Stress of Life* (Second ed.) New York: McGraw-Hill, 1978.

Silva, M. "The Delivery of Mental Health Services to Law Enforcement Officers." *Critical Incidents in Policing*, eds. J. Reese, J. Horn, and C. Dunning, rev. ed. Washington, D.C.: U.S. Government Printing Office, 1991, 335-342.

Tarcher, Jeremy P. *The Prosperity Bible: The Greatest Writings of All Time of the Secrets to Wealth and Prosperity.* New York: Penguin Group USA, 2006.

Toffler, Alvin. *Future Shock.* New York: Bantam, 1984.

Vila, Bryan. *Tired Cops: The Importance of Managing Police Fatigue.* Police Executive Research Forum. 2000.

www.ingramcontent.com/pod-product-compliance
Lightning Source LLC
Chambersburg PA
CBHW051755040426
42446CB00007B/377